ASSIGNED!
THE UNOFFICIAL AND UNAUTHORISED GUIDE TO *SAPPHIRE & STEEL*

ASSIGNED!
THE UNOFFICIAL AND UNAUTHORISED GUIDE TO *SAPPHIRE & STEEL*

RICHARD CALLAGHAN

First published in the UK in 2009 by
Telos Publishing Ltd
17 Pendre Avenue, Prestatyn, Denbighshire, LL19 9SH
www.telos.co.uk

This Edition 2013

Telos Publishing Ltd values feedback. Please e-mail us with any comments you may have about this book to: feedback@telos.co.uk

ISBN: 978-1-84583-869-0 (paperback)

British Library Cataloguing in Publication Data.
A catalogue record for this book is available from the British Library.

ACKNOWLEDGEMENTS

I would like to acknowledge my family for their support, Cheryl Burton and Will Griffin (for encouragement), Jonathan Boakes (for discussions about the series), Jim Griffin (for spotting the bit about 'the newest part of the house') and David Howe and Stephen James Walker (for helping to guide this project to completion).

The people who were kind enough to share their thoughts and reminisces were, in alphabetical order: Philip Bird, David Bishop, David Cann, David Collings, Richard Dinnick, George Douglas, Christopher Fairbank, Nigel Fairs, David Foster, Neil Guy, P J Hammond, Joseph Lidster, Anthony Read, Patricia Shakesby, Jennie Stoller, and Adrian, Russell and Terry Wootton.

All spellings of names, situations and characters have been taken from the episodes themselves and their original scripts.

CONTENTS

INTRODUCTION

Fantasy television in the late 1970s was not in a terribly good position. The BBC's flagship show, *Doctor Who,* was tending towards humour in its scripting and set-up, aiming more for a kiddie audience than the adults who had grown up with it, and there was not much else around to capture the imagination of older viewers. This was until a strange little show started airing on Tuesday and Thursday evenings. Perhaps something to do with *The Man from U.N.C.L.E.* or maybe *The New Avengers,* at least judging from its two stars, *Sapphire & Steel* was in fact a neat piece of fantasy programming. Joanna Lumley and David McCallum played the title characters, two mysterious agents, or 'time detectives' who investigated cracks in time through which terrifying creatures could break into the present. Images of the undead, faceless men and whispering, chattering darkness all terrified a generation of children and adults alike. However, its brief run and lack of terrestrial repeat screenings ensured that it perhaps remained only a half remembered nostalgia piece for the now thirty-something generation.

Ironically, it was perhaps the presence of its two stars that kept it from being as well-remembered as it deserves to be, as their CVs are collectively littered with television and film classics. Though *The New Avengers* hadn't been successful enough to warrant a third season, Lumley was making *Sapphire & Steel* in the wake of her high profile role as *The New Avengers'* Purdy. McCallum, meanwhile, had been appearing in films since the late '50s, and was infamous as *The Man from U.N.C.L.E.*'s Illya Kuryakin, a role so famous that a reunion show was broadcast the year after *Sapphire &*

Steel ended, and was even referenced in a 2005 episode of the American series *NCIS* (a show about the Naval Criminal Investigative Service). With such an enormous array of credits to their names, *Sapphire & Steel* couldn't help but go down in history as just one of many roles that the actors undertook ... the fact that the viewing public reportedly found the series inexplicable and confusing didn't help matters. During September 1989 McCallum was interviewed by Lumley on the 'Wogan' BBC chat show, where he discussed Mrs Puttock, his mother's cleaner: 'She saw the first episodes and said, "I loved it, but I didn't really understand it", so from then on in we always used to try to make the scripts Puttock proof.' Oblique, esoteric and requiring its audience to work, *Sapphire & Steel* was never about compromise or 'dumbing down'.

Looking back at the show, it's interesting to see how well it stands up to a modern day viewing. One thing that has kept the series from dating is that it has no real connection with the time in which it was made. The series is slow by modern standards, favouring atmosphere over pace, and there are some questionable hairstyles. Yet apart from the third story, there were no attempts to include overt political references in the show. As *Sapphire & Steel* began, the world was in the grip of a renewed increase in the Cold War between America and the Soviet Union, and as the series finished airing in Britain, the country was experiencing the highest level of unemployment since the 1930s. Yet none of this real-world drama finds its way onto screen and the series, which, while bleak, opts instead for self-contained fantasies, almost fairytales, that shy away from analogy. Though often cited as 'ITV's answer to *Doctor Who*' in listings magazines looking for an angle, there really was nothing else quite like *Sapphire & Steel*.

In this book, we delve into the six televised 'assignments' for the agents, looking at the continuity and backgrounds to the shows, exploring the goofs and guest stars and providing an appreciative and in depth analysis of each of the stories. I'm grateful to everyone who shared their knowledge of the show, and all unattributed quotes in the text come from interviews conducted by myself.

We also look at the ephemera which has emerged around the series, from the novelisation released at the time to the recent series of original audio plays on CD, starring David Warner as Steel and Susannah Harker as Sapphire.

So join us as we once again step into the darkness, as the mysterious control voice informs us that: 'Sapphire and Steel have been assigned ...'

PRODUCTION

Writer Peter John ('P J') Hammond had built his reputation through working on several police thrillers throughout the '60s and early '70s, including a stint as script editor on over 180 episodes of the popular *Z Cars*.

In the early '70s, he started to move into Children's telefantasy, working with Pamela Lonsdale on the popular series *Ace of Wands*. Hammond wrote three stories for this series: 'The Meddlers' (July/August 1972), 'Peacock Pie' (September 1972) and 'The Beautiful People' (November 1972). This was followed by an adaptation of Arthur Morrison's 1902 novel *The Hole in the Wall*, about a small boy in the mid-19th Century who becomes involved with his grandfather in a complex array of crimes set in the grimy east end of London, as a seven part series for the BBC transmitted in October and November 1972. In 1978 Hammond worked once more with Lonsdale as his producer, this time with 'And For My Next Trick' an episode of the anthology series *Shadows*. That same year, Lonsdale, impressed by Hammond's work, commissioned the writer to devise a stand-alone pilot for a possible television series for transmission in the children's slot between around 4.30 and 6.00pm.

Inspired after witnessing his children enjoying the George Pal cinema version of H G Wells' *The Time Machine* (1960), Hammond sent Lonsdale a proposal for a series based around time, featuring two undefined agents with a mission to protect time itself. The resulting project - *The Time Menders* - was taken by Lonsdale to Jeremy Isaacs, Head of Drama at Thames television. Unfortunately Isaacs rejected the proposed series on the grounds that he felt it lacked long-term potential.

Still enthused by the idea, Hammond took the format to Southern Television, who were interested in the story. However, Hammond was uncomfortable with their insistence that the concluding five episodes be storylined before the series was commissioned. Hammond had a working practice of writing his scripts episodically, with little documented pre-planning of where the plots would take him. While Hammond considered the offer from Southern Television's Lewis Rudd, he received an alternate offer from David Reid of ATV, agreeing to make the series on the basis of the single script.

Reid allocated the series an additional £5000 over the standard budget for a series in the timeslot and assigned Shaun O'Riordan as Producer/Director. O'Riordan was a former actor, most well known for his role as Eddie Larkin in the popular ATV series *The Larkins* (1958) and also in the spin-off film *Inn for Trouble* (1960). However, since the 1960s O'Riordan had turned to directing and producing, and had many series to his name, including *Scorpion Tales* (1978) and *Thriller* (1973-1975).

On a whim, O'Riordan sent the script for *The Time Menders* to David McCallum, little dreaming that the high profile actor who was at the time living in the United States would accept a role in a small scale British television series. McCallum thought the script was terrific, yet his fee meant that the budget allocated by David Reid was no longer viable. However, as it was an adult show, and set for transmission later in the evening, the budget could be increased to compensate. With transmission moved forward to a 7.00 pm timeslot, the presence of McCallum meant that a suitably high-profile female star would have to be cast to complement his status. Joanna Lumley, popular from her appearances as Elaine Perkins in six episodes of *Coronation Street* (1973) and more recently as Purdy in *The New Avengers* (1976-1977), was offered the part of the female agent.

The first story - now renamed *Sapphire & Steel* (and nicknamed '*Software & Steam*' by the cast) - was recorded in late 1978 at ATV's Elstree studios. Documentation listing exact dates of recording is no longer available for the series, though pre-production dates back to at least October 1978, with most of the recording scheduled for November and post-production taking place in January 1979. The script itself, as originally commissioned by Pamela Lonsdale, was aimed at the original young viewership, and featured two young children alone in a home filled with apparitions. While clues about where the agents came from and who they really were could be found in the screenplay, their full origins were deliberately kept a mystery to add to the suspense. A third agent, Lead, played by American actor Val Pringle, appeared in the latter episodes of the adventure.

The completed serial was favourably received by ATV, and a second story was commissioned to create an initial 13-part season. However, when the soap opera *Emmerdale Farm* (latterly *Emmerdale*) was scheduled to take its then regular annual break, an extra episode of *Sapphire & Steel* was commissioned to fill a seven-week period in July and August 1979, taking the initial run to 14 episodes. With the fledging series being sanctioned in stages, there was a three to four month gap between recording the two serials.

Hammond used the break to adapt the first story into a novel (which was released in paperback by Star Books to coincide with the series transmission in 1979) and to write the second. With a more ambitious plotline aimed at an older adult market, the second story was set in a railway station with more extensive sets than the first. Realising that he would need help for the extended workload, Shaun O'Riordan called on David Foster to co-direct. The two had known each other for many years as Foster had been the senior cameraman on *The Larkins*, and later performed the same role on the Charlie Drake series *The Worker*, which O'Riordan had directed. As a result the two had kept in touch. O'Riordan further noted that Foster's later work as director on the children's SF series *Timeslip* (1971) would make him an ideal candidate for a series as technically involved as *Sapphire & Steel*. They began work together on a railway station set, O'Riordan shooting all the 'downstairs/platform' sequences, while Foster handled the 'upstairs' work.

Contracted to score the series was Cyril Ornadel, a composer who had graduated from the Royal College of Music and had worked with O'Riordan earlier in the year on *Scorpion Tales*. Ornadel had been the Musical Director for London's first musical production of *My Fair Lady* in 1959, and had composed many musicals of his own. Although his background was primarily theatre, Ornadel had scored over a dozen film and television productions when he came to work on the series and his orchestral and sinister incidental music gave the series much of its edge. O'Riordan worked closely with the composer, including recording himself playing the intended theme music on a piano for Ornadel's inspiration.

The first two *Sapphire & Steel* stories were transmitted without individual titles (we have headed them 'Assignment One', 'Assignment Two' and so on for the purposes of this book) and were broadcast bi-weekly on Tuesdays and Thursdays from 10 July 1979. However, an ITV strike disrupted transmission of the second story in August 1979, and when the dispute was resolved some two months later, the story was rescreened from the start, from 30 October 1979. During the hiatus, the popular children's magazine *Look-In* launched a tie-in comic strip based on the series, a strip that was to run for 76 issues.

Despite the transmission strike, *Sapphire & Steel* was a moderate success, generally being watched by around 20% of the viewing populace, and a second, 20-part series was commissioned by ATV. Again, as with the first series, no records of production dates were kept by ATV. However, approximate times and dates of production have been gathered for this book from existing scripts, studio plans and interviews with personnel both in front of and behind the camera. It was during the first three months of 1980 that a third story went into studio, with a fourth between July and August of the same year. This time David Foster was taken on board as a regular Director, alternating with O'Riordan to balance the workload.

The third was the only story to use location footage, with scenes being shot on top of ATV's own building, and it introduced a fourth agent, Silver, played by David Collings. The most overtly political story of the series, it featured a subtext based around Hammond's belief in animal rights, something Joanna Lumley in particular was sympathetic to. The story was also the most traditionally science-fiction orientated, featuring conventional time travel, and its set-up pre-dated the *Big Brother* concept by some years, even having characters perform 'diary room' reports back to their unseen controller. As Hammond himself commented in an interview for this book, 'People say that *Sapphire & Steel* was ahead of its time in many ways, so perhaps these are further examples.'

The fourth serial is one that many people remember as being

particularly unsettling, and it revolves around a faceless man hiding in photographs to terrorise the residents of an old lost and found shop.

Transmission of the third and fourth stories was held back in the schedules until January 1981, meaning that an entire year had gone by between the initial two adventures and the third and fourth assignments. Perhaps because of this, the series recorded a slightly lower 18% average share. Two months after the fourth story was aired, *Look-In* magazine discontinued the comic strip, possibly reflecting the disruption that scheduling had done to *Sapphire & Steel*'s progression.

Although rehearsal time for the programme was lengthy, the actual recording of the episodes was done at a relatively rapid pace, with instances of episodes going into production before an entire script for the story was completed. With studio time being booked to record the fifth story immediately after the fourth, Hammond opted out due to creative exhaustion, and a replacement writer was called upon to fill the gap.

David Reid enlisted Anthony Read, an experienced writer who had worked as script editor on series including *Troubleshooters* and *Doctor Who*. As Read was concurrently working on ATV's *Hammer House Of Horror*, he saw the deadlines for *Sapphire & Steel* as being impossible to meet, and so asked another writer, Don Houghton, to work on half of the six episodes that were required. Although the two had never met, Read was aware of Houghton's work and reputation, and the two shared an agent. Houghton also had a background in telefantasy and horror, having written for *Ace of Wands* ('Now You See It, Now You Don't' (1970)), *Doctor Who* ('Inferno' (1970) and 'The Mind of Evil' (1971)) and horror, with three entries in Hammer's *Dracula* movie series (*Dracula AD 1972* (1972), *The Satanic Rites of Dracula* (1973) and *The Legend of the Seven Golden Vampires* (1974)). Given around a week to devise a plot, and less than a month in which to write it, the two authors came up with a story based on Agatha Christie's 1939 novel *Ten Little Niggers*, later retitled *And Then There Were None*, and delivered their episodes for them to be recorded around August 1980. Although the recording all went to schedule, unfortunately the transmission of the series was again sporadic: the fifth story was shown in August 1981, some six months after the fourth story had been transmitted.

P J Hammond finally scripted a four part story that served as the conclusion to the series. Recorded during November 1980, it featured a cliffhanger ending, and Hammond had vague plans to resume the story's narrative in a seventh story sometime in the future, but with the two stars (McCallum especially) having demanding work schedules elsewhere, the programme was discontinued. In December 1981, with the final story still untransmitted, ATV was defranchised by the broadcasting authorities and gave way to the newly-created Central Television. Although informal talks about the series returning took place, by the time the sixth story was eventually broadcast in August 1982, the production team and its stars had long since moved on. *Sapphire & Steel* thus took its place in television history as an arguably unique foray into fantasy, something that stands alone and seems to have few precedents or antecedents, although its influence can be determined in a number of areas.

Hammond's stock as a genre writer was in such high regard after the show ended that four years later he was commissioned by the then *Doctor Who* production team to submit a script treatment, although the resulting story, called 'Paradise Five', was ultimately rejected.

In 2006, with *Sapphire & Steel* still generally held in high regard, Hammond was in talks with regard to bringing it back to television. Although this initiative eventually petered out, that same year he was contracted to write his first fantasy script for nearly a decade, for the *Doctor Who* spin-off series *Torchwood*. The resulting episode, 'Small Worlds' (2006), featured creepy fairies and went down well enough that he was commissioned for a second, 'From Out Of The Rain' (2008). This was, as Hammond himself noted, an exploration of themes first mooted in the fourth *Sapphire & Steel* television story. It dealt with people emerging from old films to walk the earth, stealing souls into the bargain, and while seeming slightly out of place in the sexual rough and tumble of the *Torchwood* universe, was certainly redolent of Sapphire and Steel's battle with the man without a face.

With the 2005 television revival of *Doctor Who* also including such imagery as children trapped in mirrors, disembodied voices speaking through broken telephones and a town of faceless citizens, it's clear that some of the ideas and imagery from *Sapphire & Steel* have not been completely forgotten. Popular actor and writer Mark Gatiss (*The League of Gentlemen*), a noted supporter of the series, contributed a story to *Doctor Who* in 2006, 'The Idiot's Lantern', in which an alien entity trapped inside a television set 'steals' the faces of humans, leaving them looking unnervingly like the Shape from the fourth Assignment. Another of the writers for the new *Doctor Who* series, Robert Shearman, penned in 2002 a *Doctor Who* audio play, 'The Chimes of Midnight', which he confessed was a cross between *Sapphire & Steel* and *Upstairs, Downstairs*. Although the writer had watched *Doctor Who* as a child, it was *Sapphire & Steel* that had frightened him, and so he used the latter as his inspiration.

More widely in the television industry, reflections on *Sapphire & Steel* and its enigmatic nature have been mixed. Tony Jordan, a lead writer on the popular soap opera *EastEnders* and co-creator of the 2006 time travel series *Life On Mars*, cited the series as an example of a too-vague format on the BBC's Writersroom website: 'Look at some of the shows that failed in the past, something like *Sapphire & Steel*, that kind of show [...] Who are they and why are they doing what they do?' Television critic Charlie Brooker shared this view in his BBC3 series *Screenwipe*, where he showed clips from the fourth *Sapphire & Steel* story and described it as a 'wildly baffling work of metaphysical oddery.' Despite the confusion, the series is held in high regard elsewhere: Mark Gatiss once referred to Hammond as a 'genius', while another noted writer, Toby Whithouse, speaking to the BBC, acknowledged him as an influence on his own series *Being Human*: 'P J Hammond wrote *Sapphire and Steel*, which I absolutely loved. I put a gag about it in Episode Five.'

The series' standing in the printed press has also been variable. Although when first screened it received impressive coverage from the *TV Times*, retrospective views have been decidedly mixed. It was described as 'sci-fi schlock' and 'forgettable' by *The Times*, and defined as the 'highcamp Seventies counterpart' of *The X-Files* by the *Daily Mail*. Yet Mark Gatiss - who would later take a role in the *Sapphire & Steel* audio series as 'Gold' - again took time out to reference the show for a piece in the *Guardian*. Writing in 2005, he observed that in a stage production of *A Christmas Carol*, 'Scrooge is played by a man who once appeared as a very scary overgrown baby in *Sapphire & Steel*.' In 2001 Matthew Sweet of *The Independent* chose a moment from the fourth story where a woman is burnt alive in a photograph as 'the creepiest scene ever broadcast on British television'. An example of how polarising the programme's appeal could be came when *The Independent* printed two wildly different viewpoints: Liz Hunt described the series as 'dreadful' in 1996, after Stephen Poole recalled it as an 'eerie time-travel classic' the previous year.

Despite the lack of any repeats on terrestrial television, DVDs of the series have been released and, despite its modest ratings, it features frequently in retrospective survey polls. 2001 saw it reach seventh place on Channel 4's *Top Ten Sci-Fi*, the following year readers of *SFX* magazine voted it the sixth greatest British genre series, while 2004 saw it voted the fifth scariest television programme of all time in the *Radio Times*.

MAIN CAST AND CREW CREDITS

DAVID McCALLUM:
David McCallum was born in Glasgow in 1933 and is most famous for his role as the Russian spy Illya Kuryakin in *The Man From U.N.C.L.E.* (1964-1968, plus many spin-off movies and a short-lived comeback). His extensive list of roles includes parts in the films *Hell Drivers* (1957), *The Great Escape* (1963) and *The Watcher In The Woods* (1980). TV work includes *Colditz* (1972), *The Invisible Man* (1975) and *Mother Love* (1989).

The majority of McCallum's work has been in the United States, where he has appeared in numerous genre television programmes including the aforementioned *Man From U.N.C.L.E.*, *The Outer Limits* (1963/1997), *Team Knight Rider* (1997-1998) and *VR.5* (1995). From 2003 onwards he has appeared in the series *Navy NCIS: Naval Criminal Investigative Service* as Dr Donald 'Ducky' Mallard. More recently he has appeared in 67 episodes of a series called *The Replacements* (2006-2009).

JOANNA LUMLEY:
Joanna Lumley is now perhaps most well-known for her role as Patsy Stone in the sitcom *Absolutely Fabulous*, which originally ran from 1992-1995. After the series finished as a regular production, its popularity led to first a 1996 special, then a full resurrection of the series in 2001. The last edition to date was a *Comic Relief* special in 2005.

Lumley was born in 1946, in Kashmir, India to a Major in the Gurkhas, and lived there until her teens. Failing a RADA audition aged 16, she became a model until getting work in small parts for projects like *The Bruce Forsyth Show* (1966) and the James Bond film *On Her Majesty's Secret Service* (1969). Larger roles followed, including a memorable part as Harold Steptoe's girlfriend in an episode of *Steptoe and Son* (1972) and Elaine Perkins in six episodes of *Coronation Street* (1973).

Lumley's most famous role pre-Patsy was as Purdy in *The New Avengers* (1976-1977), and the actress has also appeared in numerous high-profile television commercials. With her career once more in ascendance since the early '90s, many television roles have been built around her, including *Girl Friday* (1994), *Dr Willoughby* (1999) and *Sensitive Skin* (2005, 2007). Lumley has recently appeared in, and lent her voice to, several children's films, including *James and The Giant Peach* (1996), *The Magic Roundabout* and *Corpse Bride* (both 2005).

DAVID COLLINGS:

Probably the most famous guest actor in terms of his roles in the genre, David Collings appeared three times in *Doctor Who* ('Revenge of the Cybermen' (1975), 'The Robots of Death' (1977) and 'Mawdryn Undead' (1983)), and had a role in 'Blake', the final episode of *Blake's 7* (1981). Collings could also be seen in two episodes of *Out Of The Unknown:* 'Level 7' (1966) and 'The Naked Sun' (1969), as well as an episode of *UFO*: 'The Psychobombs' (1970). One of Collings' earliest television roles after *Sapphire & Steel* ended was as a prosecutor in *Them And Us* (1985), significant because he was once more directed by David Foster.

Born in June 1940, Collings had been appearing on television for 15 years before his role as Silver, debuting in 'Moving On' (March 1965), an edition of *The Wednesday Play*. Collings could also be seen as the character Mr Winters in five episodes of *Press Gang* from 1989 to 1993, though the thirtysomething generation perhaps owes him its greatest debt with his voiceover talents as the lead character for the English dubbed version of *Saiyūki* (1979-1981), otherwise known as *Monkey*.

Now in his late sixties, Collings continues to work, largely in the theatre, including in a world tour of *Troilus and Cressida* in 2008. Recent years have seen him working with the audio production company Big Finish, including playing an alternate Doctor in *Doctor*

Who Unbound: Full Fathom Five (2003) and reprising his role of Silver for their *Sapphire & Steel* range of audios.

P J HAMMOND:

Peter John Hammond had studied arts and drama, but began his preferred career as a writer by selling plays to radio stations. Moving into television by writing for the BBC Schools department, his commissions increased via children's drama (including *Ramshackle Road* and *Adventure Weekly*) and then into police detective series. Script editor on *Z-Cars* from 1968-1970, Hammond also contributed scripts and worked on episodes of, amongst others, *New Scotland Yard* (1972), *Hazell* (1978), *Dixon of Dock Green* (1974) and *The Sweeney* (1976). It was this mix of small screen detection, coupled with his occasional forays into surreal children's programming (*Shadows, Ace of Wands*) that inspired the detective-series-with-a-twist that was *Sapphire & Steel.*

Post-*Sapphire & Steel* Hammond's work reverted back into the traditional detective genre, with writing credits on *The Gentle Touch, The Bill* and *Unnatural Causes* throughout the 1980s. The 1990s and 2000s saw him craft further episodes of *The Bill,* as well as episodes of *Doctor Finlay, Dangerfield, Wycliffe* and *Midsomer Murders,* while a return to the SF genre occurred in 1998 with *Space Island One* and then in 2006/2008 with episodes for the *Doctor Who* spin-off, *Torchwood.* Perhaps most notable of Hammond's post-*Sapphire & Steel* works is *Lame Ducks,* his only other 'creator' credit. A six-part sitcom about a man (John Duttine) opting out of society to join his own commune, it aired on BBC2 during the winter of 1984. Produced and Directed by John B Hobbs, the comedy also featured Lorraine Chase and Brian Murphy, and - while not particularly well remembered - was deemed successful enough to be recommissioned for a second six-part series on the same channel the following year.

ANTHONY READ:

Anthony Read began his television writing career in the 1960s, working on *Z-Cars,* and then acting as script editor on *Detective* (1964), *The Indian Tales of Rudyard Kipling* (1964) and *The Troubleshooters* (1965-1966). Later he would go on to write and produce *The Troubleshooters* (1966-1969) before moving on to programmes like the BBC's *Play For Today* (1971).

In the late '70s he acted as script editor on *Doctor Who* (1977-1979) and wrote the Tom Baker story *The Horns of Nimon* (1979/1980) as well as co-writing *The Invasion of Time* (1978) for the same actor. In 1980, while contracted to write a *Sapphire & Steel* story in Hammond's absence, Read was simultaneously the script editor on *Hammer House of Horror*. Other genre works included adapting the John Wyndham novels for the television series *Chocky* (1984) and its follow-ups, *Chocky's Children* (1985) and *Chocky's Challenge* (1986).

One of Read's most famous writing assignments was for the BBC's *The Baker Street Boys* (1983), a series for which he wrote a number of spin-off novels. Though Read continued to write for television well into the late 1990s, he began to branch out into book writing more frequently, often writing non-fiction centred around World War II. To this day Read is primarily a print author, occasionally writing prose fiction.

DON HOUGHTON:

Don Houghton began writing for radio in 1951 before moving into television in the late 1950s. Among his television credits he was the creator of Scottish soap *Take The High Road* (1980-2003), writer then script editor on episodes of *The Flaxton Boys* (1969/1970) and writer of the two Jon Pertwee *Doctor Who* stories *Inferno* (1970) and *The Mind of Evil* (1971).

However Houghton was perhaps most well known for his film work with Hammer Productions, where he wrote the screenplays for *Dracula A.D. 1972* (1972), *The Satanic Rites of Dracula* (1973) and *The Legend of the 7 Golden Vampires* (1974). Houghton also acted as Producer on the last two movies. In 1986 he returned to writing for Hammer on the small screen with 'Black Carrion' an episode of *Hammer House of Mystery and Suspense* (1986).

In 1980 he co-wrote a *Sapphire & Steel* story with Anthony Read, as well as having writing credits on television programmes as diverse as *The Doombolt Chase* (1978), *Ace of Wands* (1970) and *The Professionals* (1978/1979). Houghton passed away in 1991.

SHAUN O'RIORDAN:

Shaun O'Riordan started working in television as an actor,

appearing in seventeen episodes of *The Adventures of Robin Hood* from 1956 to 1957. He also played Jake O'Dowd in *Emergency-Ward 10* (1957), though was most famous playing Eddie Larkin in *The Larkins* (1958-1964) and its spin-off feature film, *Inn For Trouble* (1960).

He gave up acting to take up producing and directing, working in comedy, such as on the Charlie Drake vehicle *The Worker* (1965-1970), and with Sid James and Peggy Mount in *George and the Dragon* (1966-1968). His comedy Producer (and occasional Director) credits include *You're Only Young Twice* (1971) and *The Squirrels* (1974-1976).

He worked on *Softly, Softly, Thriller* and *General Hospital.* O'Riordan produced the 1984 sitcom *I Thought You'd Gone* and produced and directed the *Callan* sequel *Wet Job* (1981) as well as the 1985 sitcom *Trouble and Strife.*

SEASON ONE

ASSIGNMENT ONE

EPISODE	UK TRANSMISSION	TIME	DURATION	AUDIENCE SHARE
ONE	Tue: 10 Jul 1979	19:00	25'41m	23%
TWO	Thur: 12 Jul 1979	19:00	24'26m	22%
THREE	Tue: 17 Jul 1979	19:00	23'52m	22%
FOUR	Thur: 19 Jul 1979	19:00	24'55m	22%
FIVE	Tue: 24 Jul 1979	19:00	24'35m	22%
SIX	Thur: 26 Jul 1979	19:00	24'43m	21%

GUEST CAST:
Steven O'Shea (Rob), Tamasin Bridge (Helen), Val Pringle (Lead), Felicity Harrison (Mother), John Golightly (Father), Ronald Goodale (Countryman), Les Clark (Victorian Man, uncredited), Rex Browne and George Romanov (Ironside Troopers, uncredited) and Charles Pemberton (Policeman).

TECHNICAL PERSONNEL:
Mike Whitcutt (Cameras), Neil Guy (Vision Mixer), John Hawkins (VTR Editor), Mary Southgate (Make-Up), Ann Murphy (Stage Manager), Len Penfold (Sound), Jim Reeves (Vision Control), Dawn Evans (Wardrobe), Ron Brown (Programme Administrator), Sean O'Farrell (Floor Manager), Joyce Lewsey (Production Assistant), Ivor Weir (Title Sequence), Cyril Ornadel (Music), Jim Boyers (Lighting), Stanley Mills (Designer), David Reid (Executive Producer), P J Hammond (Creator/Writer) and Shaun O'Riordan (Director/Producer). An ATV Network Production.

SYNOPSIS:

Henry and Sarah Jardine live with their two children in a house built in 1736. Henry's collection of antique clocks and their daughter Helen's historical nursery rhymes cause enough of a clash of time periods for intangible creatures to break through a crack in time and occupy the house. All clocks in the house stop and the two parents vanish, leaving their son, Rob, to telephone the police. Instead he and Helen are confronted by two strangers known as Sapphire and Steel, who explain that they have been assigned to get their parents back. Using various special powers to try to defeat the creatures that lurk in the corners of the house, they are soon joined by a third agent, Lead, in order to complete their mission. After the creatures take hold of Rob in the cellar, the agents defeat them by luring them into the oldest stone laid in the house, then freezing the stone and destroying it. Sapphire, Steel and Lead say their goodbyes as the parents are returned and time is restored.

TIME AND THE UNKNOWN:

Explaining how the mechanics of the series would work, Sapphire and Steel note: 'There is a corridor. And the corridor is time. It surrounds all things and it passes through all things. Sometimes time can break in and take things. And people [...] There are creatures from the very beginnings of time and the very ends of time. They have access to the corridor and are forever searching for tears in the fabric in order to gain access.'

PAST ASSIGNMENTS:

At some time before this first story, Sapphire and Steel worked on a mission aboard the *Mary Celeste*. Although there is no date is specified, there are several hints that this adventure was recent, possibly even just before they came to the house, with no break in between (cv. Steel: 'Rob... you remember the first time we came here, came to this house? [...] I'm sorry I was so rude. It's just that I'd had a difficult time, a bad time in that ship.') Of this earlier mission, we learn that Lead had to join them for a single day, where they left a replica of the *Mary Celeste* behind, having sunk the original 'for its own good.'

The evolution of the enemies the agents face can be seen through the progression from this unseen story to the one shown on screen. Over the course of the series we see the creatures develop from a simple patch of light into a full mass of darkness, through to animal and then human form, and finally to a higher power. (The only divergence from this progression is the fifth story, not written by Hammond, which features just an 'entity'.) We learn that the creature on board the *Mary Celeste* was triggered by an out-of-date ship's log and was unintelligent. Steel notes here, 'This time it can think, it can reason things out.' Sapphire also comments on their current mission that, 'most of [the creature's effect] is history gone wrong. We've never had that before.' Sapphire also tells Rob that she saw a break in time on board the ship, 'like frosted glass.'

Sapphire shows Rob illusions of clothes she'd worn previously. These include lemon and red ball gowns. In both cases she was a brunette, suggesting further earlier adventures for her.

FUTURE ASSIGNMENTS:

Lead informs Sapphire when he arrives: 'There's another difficult [mission] waiting for us. When we've finished here, of course.' As Lead did not appear in any other televised episodes, we can assume that this was an unscreened Assignment.

SAPPHIRE AND STEEL:

We learn that Sapphire and Steel are agents whose mission is to stop time breaking in and disrupting the present. They share the power of telepathy, although their application of it possibly varies. Sapphire is shown to be able to read minds as well as project her thoughts, whereas it's implied that Steel can monitor her thoughts without her having to transfer them. After Rob deceives Sapphire by telling her that Steel asked for her, Steel's immediate telepathic response is 'I sent no message' – this from two storeys up and without Sapphire having to ask him or relay what the situation was.

Their powers and methods are diverse, Sapphire being described by Steel as the 'diplomat' and having the empathic ability to sense the age of objects. She can unlock doors with the power of her mind and can also repeat cycles in time. However, the time scale she can take back is limited, though it is at least half a day. In the third episode she asks for Steel's help in taking back time. Whether his power aids the process or he is acting merely as moral support is unspecified, though such a feat drains Steel and causes him to drop to his knees afterwards. Finally, Sapphire's ability to play with time allows her to project the illusion of garments and hair colours she has worn in the past. Lead suggests that the difficulty of their Assignment would be 'good training' for Sapphire, which perhaps suggests that she's relatively new at the job.

As well as his telepathic abilities, Steel is able to drastically reduce his body temperature. In episode three he reduces it to -273.20°. However, to help him survive, he is advised to use Lead as insulation. An indication that the two have never been human is given when Rob says to Steel, 'Don't you know your history?' 'I know mine,' claims Steel.

OLD BLUE EYES IS BACK:
When Sapphire uses her powers, her eyes usually glow blue and a pulsating sound effect is heard. Her power is used seven times throughout the story, and the first time her eyes glow a dark blue. Thereafter (and usually throughout the other stories) it's a medium blue, save for the final time when the effect isn't used at all, and her eyes remain their original brown. Twice in addition to the 'pulsating' noise there's a more traditional SF sound effect overlaid when Sapphire uses her powers. This secondary sound effect was used again in only one other *Sapphire & Steel* story.

'HELP ME, STEEL!':
While *Sapphire & Steel* was a fairly progressive programme for its time, there are many instances where Sapphire would be called upon to play the role of 'damsel in distress'. The first story features in episode three a wonderful example of surrealism, where Sapphire is absorbed into a cottage room via a painting.

THE ELEMENTS:
We find out during the course of the story that there are 127 elements in total, including 12 transuranics. Steel warns against counting the transuranics, claiming 'They're unstable'. The show's title sequence informs us that the transuranics are 'not available where there is life'. Transuranic elements in chemical science are artificial elements with a greater atomic number than 92. They all have a short life span that are all radioactive – which would explain their non usage around living creatures.

This is one of only two stories where we get to hear about the unseen agents, with a tantalising description of three of the other elements from the titles. Jet is identified as female, and Lead notes that she 'sends her love' to Steel. We also learn that Copper is 'having problems' - presumably relationship problems - with Silver.

Lead is a black, American-accented male of around 6'5" tall, possessing considerable physical strength and the ability to act as insulation. A gregarious character, his relationship with Sapphire is affectionate, though Steel is less tolerant of him, possibly because he needs Lead to effectively perform sub-zero feats when he feels that he should be able to cope on his own. Lead's light-hearted attitude to their missions is responsible for angering the more business-like Steel. When Lead claims the creatures in the house are very organised, Steel responds: 'Maybe you could learn something from them.' While we can presume that Lead has a level of telepathic communication with the other agents, this isn't shown on screen.

STRANGE RELATIONSHIP:

Throughout the series there are occasional hints of a romantic attraction between Sapphire and Steel, though these are more fleeting allusions, rather than overt references. In charting this somewhat underplayed subtext of the series, it's important to note that it was intentional, and P J Hammond was fully aware of it: 'I liked their flirting and the suggestion that there could have been something between them at one time. I believe it's important to maintain the air of mystery.'

For this first story, Steel is introduced rather obliquely by Sapphire as 'my friend', while on two occasions he speaks to her with his face unusually close to hers, her eyes flickering up and down as he speaks. The first episode sees Steel place his hand on Sapphire's right shoulder, with her placing her hand on his. Sapphire also rather abashedly apologises to Steel for misusing her powers in order to show Rob the trick with her clothes.

When Lead tells Steel that Jet 'sends her love', he looks annoyed, while Sapphire appears amused.

Finally, it's worth documenting a confrontation in the kitchen during the fifth episode where Steel is being unnecessarily harsh to Rob and Helen. Sapphire makes him feel guilty, and gives him an accusing look. Steel apologises, then walks away smiling.

YOU MAY REMEMBER ME FROM ...

VAL PRINGLE:
More famous in the United States where he was born in 1937, Val Pringle appeared in five films, including *Shoot It Black, Shoot It Blue* (1974), *The Last Remake of Beau Geste* (1977) and *Ragtime* (1981). He also appeared in an episode of *The Professionals*, credited as Valentine Pringle.

Heavily rooted in the stage tradition, Pringle also earned a living as a songwriter, probably his most famous composition being 'Louise', which was recorded by Harry Belafonte as a track on his 1970 album *The Warm Touch*. In the 1980s Pringle moved with his wife to Lesotho, Africa. In December 1999 he was killed while trying to apprehend burglars at his home.

MISSION BRIEF:
It's frequently noted that, scientifically speaking, sapphire and steel aren't actually elements at all. Steel is possibly forgivable as it is an alloy of two elements – primarily iron, with a small proportion of carbon. Sapphire, however, is a chemical compound. The names referenced in the title sequence that actually *are* elements are: Gold (atomic number 79), Lead (82), Copper (29), Radium (88), Silver (47) and Diamond (a form of carbon) (6). Jet is also composed primarily of carbon.

P J Hammond originally intended that there would be only two agents seen in the series. The concept of Sapphire and Steel being just two of many was suggested to him by Shaun O'Riordan.

Hammond cited H G Wells, Ray Bradbury, Nigel Kneale and J B Priestley as influences on his *Sapphire & Steel* writing.

Much of the background to the title agents is still surrounded in mystery, not least where they come from, and what they actually are. Hammond maintains that this was deliberate: 'I really think it's part of the mystery not to know where they came from. Not knowing has never bothered me, and I believe it did no harm to the storytelling. I've never been fond of exposition, especially when writing fantasy.'

Possibly the biggest mystery surrounding the programme is

the identity of the narrator of the title sequence. A myth that the voice belonged to actor David Suchet has been dispelled by Shaun O'Riordan, though he keeps the real identity of the speaker a secret. Speculation as to why this might be so was given by fellow director David Foster: 'I am fairly sure it was Shaun O'Riordan's voice. As he was a professional actor with an Equity ticket, for such a short sequence, it made sense.'

The narration and music to the opening title sequence was devised by O'Riordan, who recorded the trial version himself on a piano. With different wording for the first rough take (which can be heard on the Region 1 DVD release), one of the first agents named was 'Granite'.

There are 17 clocks seen in the house throughout the story. Vision mixer Neil Guy recalled of David McCallum from his time on set: 'He was very aware of continuity, and in the story where many clocks featured when they were moving back and forward in time, he saved the day more than once by noticing that a certain clock on the set wasn't showing the correct (story) time.'

The electronic effect known as chromakey was used to achieve the sequences of Sapphire's eyes glowing blue, her normal eye colour replaced with a blue light. Dating back to 1940, chromakey was a system of blending two images together using a colour-keyed reference. This process is also often called Colour Separation Overlay (CSO), or 'green screen'.

When Lead's hand freezes after touching Steel in the final episode, actor Val Pringle had his hand already made up to look 'frozen' and hid it from view until it was required.

There are five nursery rhymes used in this story: 'Little Miss Muffet' (16th Century); 'Ring-A-Ring of Roses' (indefinite origin, first printed 1881), 'Goosey Goosey Gander' (18th Century); 'The North Wind Doth Blow' (16th Century) and 'The House That Jack Built' (1755). Also featured in the story is the popular sea shanty 'What Shall We Do With The Drunken Sailor?', which, like the rhymes, is part of an oral tradition and so cannot be accurately sourced as to its origin. However, the first printed publication of the music for the song was c. 1824-1825, with the lyrics being first printed in 1891.

As discussed in the introduction to this book, no records of production were kept by ATV, leaving the recording dates in doubt.

However, design plans for the attic bedroom and the father's office list scheduled 'VTR Dates' as 6-7 November 1978, while a special effects requirement sheet dated 27/10/1978 also lists the same period. A camera script for episode three cites the VTR date as '23rd/24th November, 1978' with an edit on the same episode for 7th January and sound dub on 30th January 1979.

GOOFS:

There's a slight continuity clash nine-and-a-half minutes into the fourth episode: Rob is seen through the stairway, sat talking to Helen with his hands crossed above his lap and his cardigan open. The picture cuts to a medium long shot from the side, with Rob's hands lower down and his cardigan done up.

The 'dusk skyline' that Rob stands in front of during the final episode is very clearly a backdrop, with noticeable stretch marks on the material.

Finally, look out for the fourth cliffhanger. Not only is the 'floating page' very obviously manipulated by a fishing line, but Tamasin Bridge appears to be breaking into unscripted giggles.

THE CLIFFHANGERS:

- EPISODE ONE: Helen begins to recite 'Ring-A-Ring of Roses' to herself, causing the presence to emerge in her bedroom and locking out Steel …
- EPISODE TWO: Rob begins to say the nursery rhyme 'Goosey Goosey Gander' against his will. As he does so, Roundhead soldiers appear on the stairs and break open the door to Helen's room …
- EPISODE THREE: Steel freezes the portrait, causing Sapphire to be released. However, in doing so, the Roundhead soldiers are also freed …
- EPISODE FOUR: A page from Helen's book of nursery rhymes escapes being burnt, causing chaos to once more break out around the house. Sapphire and Helen try and catch the page as a window shatters and winds rage through the kitchen …
- EPISODE FIVE: In an attempt to locate Rob, Sapphire and Steel are blocked by a heavy wooden door to the cellar, which they inform Lead is locked. 'It isn't now,' replies

Lead, breaking it off its hinges with one shove.

OVERVIEW:

The first story presented by *Sapphire & Steel* has the perfect elements to terrify a young audience. While it - and the series as a whole - may seem a little slow by modern standards, it portrays very effectively the scenario of a young boy, Rob, played by the very capable Steven O'Shea, being surrounded by growing psychological terror. In the 21st Century, when TV drama is often served up as a mix of jump cuts and characters verbalising their emotions, *Sapphire & Steel*'s stock-in-trade mix of brooding atmosphere, mannered performances and the unexplained may be off-putting to new viewers, or possibly just a dying art.

P J Hammond cleverly - almost irresponsibly - plays on the most base and primal of a child's fears and allows them to build. One of the first shots is of the darkness outside the large house (a very impressive set), a tree branch tapping on the window. We then learn that the child's parents have vanished in mysterious circumstances. Rob's younger sister Helen (Tamasin Bridge, the weakest aspect of the opening story) is too young to fully understand the situation, though the added responsibility in the face of uncertainty it forces upon Rob adds to the tension. Lest Helen's indifference to the danger distract, composer Cyril Ornadel amplifies the sense of the unknown with arguably his best score for the series.

Yet it doesn't end there. Soon the knowledge that the house is deserted for miles around and without communication is subtly imparted - 'I ran all the way to the phone box at Scar's Edge. Telephoned the policeman's house at the point. [...] He'll only have to come out to the other side of the point and cross the bay in a boat and he'll be here.' Any possibility of easing off on the tension is taken away by the presence of Sapphire and Steel, two aloof strangers who arrive instead of the policeman, cloaked in shadows and claiming they're the only ones who can help. Just when things seem to reach a vague level of comfort with Sapphire's maternal nature coming to the fore, the story opens out into a full-blown ghost tale, with disembodied knocking, creaking doors that open by themselves and horrific apparitions.

While it doesn't have as many layers and subtexts as the

following stories for adult viewers to appreciate (being written very much as it was originally intended to be, an intelligent children's drama), for a young viewer, this is almost undoubtedly the scariest episode of them all. 'Scary' was one of the things *Sapphire & Steel* was most noted for, being broadcast at a time when science fiction on television was being typified by a more humorous approach from cult favourite *Doctor Who* and glitsy fare from America like *Buck Rogers in the 25th Century*. *Sapphire & Steel* saw out the '70s and early '80s with stories that were early evening horror, the very epitome of parental guidance viewing. In this story, children are the victims, the focal point for the audience, and innocent nursery rhymes are the incantations used to bring forth spirits of the dead.

Some of the nursery rhymes featured aren't as historically sinister as they would first appear - the popular belief that 'Ring-A-Ring of Roses' refers to the Plague, for example, has been largely discredited, as the first record of the rhyme's existence was in 1881, some 200 years later - yet they're haunting all the same. As in all good horror, it's the everyday given a touch of the macabre that brings a chill, and having familiar rhymes chanted menacingly by ghosts (or 'visual refractions' as Sapphire would have them) brings that horror right into the personal domain of children.

It has to be acknowledged that it's not all pitch-perfect terror. The second episode's shot of a flying teddy bear in a dress is unintentionally hysterical, as is the page of the book later in the story, very obviously manipulated by a fishing line. And perhaps it was somewhat cruel of the producers, given that O'Shea had trouble pronouncing his Rs, that he still had to give the policeman's name as 'Brian Trelawney' at the dramatic climax. But this was sinister, unsettling stuff for 1979, and even though the second half of the story may get a little 'safe' with the presence of Lead, having Tamasin Bridge play her character as a corpse in a coffin perhaps indicates that wasn't a television series that was prepared to compromise.

One unusual subtext for a family serial is Rob's obvious infatuation with Sapphire. Many shots see him gazing adoringly at her (at one point he tells her 'I just think that you're beautiful'), while in the first episode she openly flirts with him to gain his trust. Rob's reaction toward the two interlopers as temporary substitute parents sees him take on an almost Oedipal relationship to Steel, and it's only in the fourth episode that he briefly gets chance to play like a child.

While writing the first season of *Sapphire & Steel*, P J Hammond was also contracted to turn out a novelisation of this first story, aimed at the younger market. This was something he wasn't naturally comfortable with. ('I would not be happy writing [audio stories],' he later said, 'because I can only think of the series as a visual experience. The same applies to writing a *Sapphire & Steel* novel.') The novelisation is nevertheless of interest, primarily because Hammond expands on Rob's feelings of adolescent attraction toward Sapphire. He puts Helen at six years old, and Rob about to enter puberty at 12. A particular passage observes: '[Rob] accepted [Sapphire] and he was fascinated by her, but he could not trust her. Not yet. And, because of the young, and therefore strange, feelings that he had for her, she would be the last person to see him weep. Perhaps later, in the privacy of his own room, and in his own bed, he would allow himself the painful but necessary luxury of crying.' Rob's attraction to Sapphire even prompts him to increased bravery; while in the first two episodes he flees and cowers from the apparitions, when these same apparitions attack Sapphire at the end of the third, he hurtles up the stairs to rescue her.

Of the two leads, Lumley is sparky and engaging, even though her Sapphire is less proactive and more of a traditionalised female figure than she would later become. (Notable Sapphire activities in this opening story include looking after the children, cooking and cleaning.) McCallum's Steel is another matter entirely: a TV original as a taciturn, bad tempered - almost cruel - and intense man. His heavy-handed yanking of Helen's chin borders on sadism, as does his forcefully scornful questioning: 'What do you think it would do? Scurry back up the stairs to mum for a bit of comfort? Hang on to her the same way you've been hanging on to Sapphire?'. With the series frequently recorded around McCallum's busy schedule, it is notable that in the first and final stories his hair is considerably shorter than in the other four, forfeiting the vaguely androgynous motif he and Lumley occasionally share in the latter.

The other agent seen in the story is Lead. Val Pringle is immensely likeable in the role, but Lead was written as a standard 'strong man', not specifically a black man, or an American. Lead's first line of dialogue is, 'Hello, Sapphire. Got anything to eat in this place? […] You know what, I'm starving!' and it doesn't improve from there. Pringle gets no fewer than 16 opportunities to laugh heartily, often with little to no provocation. On the surface, the character doesn't work in the universe of *Sapphire & Steel*. The pace and tone of the story sees McCallum and Lumley delivering their lines in a deliberately mannered, stilted way. Lead's presence threatens to undermine the entire structure as his booming bass voice and naturalistic phrasing jar with this. Maybe the fundamental problem with Lead is that not only does he not share the moral ambiguities of the other characters but Val Pringle's performance style contrasts so remarkably with David McCallum's understated reading. Consequently it's possible to say that Pringle almost *over*acts McCallum off the screen, though their scenes together do amuse and charm by contrast. Of course, another reading is that each of the agents has been written, and is performed by the actor, to reflect his 'element' and the different emotional responses that it can generate. Thus Sapphire is beautiful and serene, with hidden depths, is caring and maternal, is the sensitive, loving side. Steel on the other hand is stand-alone, hard and forceful, doing what needs to be done even if people might get hurt in the process. Following this train of thought, Lead is strong and invincible so he laughs at the world, has a carefree approach as nothing can hurt him, and finds fun in situations that cause others to cower.

The humour present in the story is bleak, almost gallows humour, as will become customary for the series. One tense moment sees Sapphire gazing at a meat cleaver that's about to be used to decapitate her after a rendition of 'Goosey Goosey Gander'. 'You could have settled for "Oranges and Lemons"', she quips. Another rare moment of amusement is Steel's punning assertion that the Transuranics are 'unstable'. While Lead's status can be argued (even insofar as his American roots), at no point in the story is his skin colour referenced, not even by the children who are called upon to describe him. (He is 'almost a giant,' they say.) While his physical nature fits that of his element, there is no explicit comparison drawn between the two, and no real indication that Pringle was cast for this reason. (Hammond's novelisation strips the character down further in terms of development and describes him thus: 'This huge man was dark blue. Like ink.') What Lead's presence does is cement the Elements into a more humanised context, where presumably all the accents of Earth are or could be represented. This begs the question whether or not the elements were originally human, something also brought into focus by Steel sleeping (a factor that will be contradicted by the following story) and Lead eating and drinking (an occurrence that will make the series' finale problematic).

A notable aspect of the production is that there are long stretches of silence used to create mood. By the time *Sapphire & Steel* reached its final story, Cyril Ornadel's music would be almost ubiquitous, but here it's used sparingly. The production all round, in fact, is solid, with only the 'exteriors' of the final episode palling somewhat, still made palatable by Jim Boyers' superb lighting. This is a television series so involved in its own mythology and sense of style that it frequently has its main stars in silhouette. Many of the ideas and concepts involved are verbal, such as Steel's discussion about the beginnings and ends of time, a highly evocative means of stirring the audience's imaginations without having to invest in expensive effects.

If there's one way in which the first Assignment doesn't live up to its full potential, it's that the second half of the story has too many narrative divergences, the final episode often not possessing the atmosphere that made the first half so special. The reason for this was that Hammond disliked developing story treatments, and wrote an episode at a time, often not knowing where the plot would go from one week to the next, or how it would be resolved. While this isn't especially obvious in later serials, the fast development pace of the series - being produced as Hammond was still writing - means that the writer's hand can often be felt, if only in the need to introduce a third agent halfway through.

Sapphire & Steel was a television series that - particularly in its first season - was concerned with allowing a story to flow naturally, rather than introducing a number of artificial dramatic 'highs'. As a result, many of the 'cliffhangers' in this first Assignment aren't climatic hooks enticing the viewer to watch the next instalment, but functional adjuncts to the action. A good case in point is the final one, which sees Lead break down a door and then abruptly halts as the episode's running time has expired. No real attempt is made to express a further danger lurking beyond the door - although we know that Rob is in trouble below, the final shot lingers on the whimsy of Lead's feat of strength. This problem with the cliffhangers is further illustrated by the inclusion of three virtually identical, albeit effective, ones, all involving Roundhead soldiers.

An indication that Hammond himself was dissatisfied with the final scripts for the serial perhaps comes with the novelisation. The final two episodes take up less than a quarter of the book, and the third episode little more than a tenth - an indicator of which episodes Hammond regarded as having genuine depth and content. The hurried production and lack of storylining unfortunately mean that there are some contradictions in the plot. The final episode has Sapphire, after spending most of the story searching for the elusive patches of light, able to make them reveal themselves at will by using her powers. A possible get-out is that the approximate location of the creatures is known at that time, but was not earlier. However, there is no explanation for why the newest part of the house is stated in episode two to be the extension ... yet four episodes later it's claimed to be Helen's bedroom. This is not to mention the fact that the story often doesn't make sense by *Sapphire & Steel*'s own remit. Considering that the series is supposedly about 'triggers' allowing time to break through, it is surprising that only in the fourth story does this genuinely take place. Neither of the first two stories has any realistically-defined 'triggers'; Steel's explanation of a family with an old name saying an old nursery rhyme in an old house is unsuitably vague here. The implication seems to be that time has enough weak points for creatures to emerge through without the need for any trigger ... but that a trigger will attract the creature to a certain point when it has arrived.

Continuing the theme of things not quite adding up, Sapphire's explanation of an ashtray possibly drawing the creature because 'there are some recycled elements there; one of them's a good hundred years old' seems to ignore the fact that all objects are composed of older materials. This means that the series' own rules have undermined it, because by definition *anything* can be the trigger. Yet the moments of genuine terror for the younger age group mean that Assignment One manages to bypass such logistical flaws by virtue of its confident style and originality.

There are some moments in the story that are very much of

the time - Steel only has to tell the policeman who has travelled over the bay to investigate a missing persons case that he's a 'friend of the family' for him to be satisfied. Then there's the appearance of a Golliwog doll in Helen's room. The Golliwogg (spelt with two 'g's) is attributed as the creation of Florence Upton in 1895 (so it does, ironically, fit in with the story's Victorian childhood subtext). Upton wrote a story based around a Minstrel rag doll she had played with as a child, effectively creating an outrageous caricature of what was already an outrageous caricature. By the 1980s, the doll had fallen from favour, and the name become associated more with racism than with childhood. Its appearance in a *Sapphire & Steel* story shows no political leanings, but merely freezes it as a snapshot of the time when such toys were commonplace in many households.

As the series progressed, Hammond would introduce greater elements of surrealism (the plight of Sapphire being absorbed into a painting is taken to its fullest degree in the fourth story) and increase the powers of the two main characters. In this first Assignment, we see Sapphire manipulating time and Steel taking his body temperature down close to absolute zero - an idea not used again - and a demonstration of the power of telepathy between the two. The concept of telepathy is an interesting feature, introduced casually 12 minutes into the first episode, purely as a means of communication between the two leads. Probably the most intriguing aspect of this comes in the following episode, where Rob attempts to deceive Sapphire. 'I sent no message', Steel telepathically relays from two floors up. As Sapphire hadn't asked the question, the implication can only be that Steel is monitoring the conversation from afar … possibly through Sapphire, with them possessing some form of shared mind. In Hammond's novelisation he gives a tantalising glimpse of how he perceived the power, in the moment where Rob tries to deceive Sapphire: 'If Rob could have tapped the atmosphere, or the mind-waves, or had the insight and the power to avoid looking the subconscious in the eye, he might have got away with it.' However, the idea of the agents having the power of ESP was actually a late suggestion by Shaun O'Riordan (along with the inclusion of other agents and Sapphire's blue eyes) after Hammond's original script had them talking in whispered asides.

First named as such in 1882 by Fredric W H Myers, a founder of the Society for Psychical Research (an organisation of which the character George Tully will claim to be a member in the following Assignment), telepathy wasn't a particularly original concept for the genre, even in that period on TV, with *Blake's 7*'s Cally doing the same thing over on BBC One between 1978 and 1981.[1] The difference is, whereas most telepaths in television science fiction, or even literature, can seem somewhat 'gimmicky', here the concept is developed into a brilliantly clever conceit by Hammond in order to deliver exposition. While this might seem the ultimate in gimmicks, the reliance upon telepathy means that it's never presented as a throwaway get-out that is discarded and picked up as and when the writer needs it to help him out of a tight corner; it's always present.

The concluding episode - hastily written by Hammond and then reworked by O'Riordan and McCallum uncredited - adopts some shaky logic and is perhaps too complex for the primary audience. However, while the focal point of the story does seem to drift away in the second half, one notable plus is that Hammond was aware of the actual broadcast time midway through writing. Rather than going out in a pre-6.00 pm kids' slot as with shows like *Ace of Wands* and *The Tomorrow People*, it was scheduled for a 7.00 pm slot on weekday evenings. This gave Hammond leeway to include more adult material, and is perhaps reflected in the further increase in horror, with the clones of Rob and Helen's parents, and indeed the corpse of Helen lying in a coffin. While the very obviously painted eyes of the mother might distract, the serial employs two techniques that would be used to such rewarding effect in *The Blair Witch Project* 21 years later. The first is an unsettling sequence recorded with a hand-held camera and featuring a direct point of view shot of Rob looking into the lens as he follows his father down the cellar stairs. The second is a positively chilling moment when Rob's mother is speaking with her

---

[1] Allusions to telepathy occurred in literary science fiction even before the term was coined: G H Ryan's *Fifteen Months In The Moon* (1880) featured the concept, and Fitz-James O'Brien's *The Bohemian*, written before 1862 and eventually published in 1885, had a girl who possessed ESP under hypnosis. Probably the most highly regarded of all literature featuring telepathy is the first recipient of the Hugo Award, Alfred Bester's *The Demolished Man* (1953).

back turned to him, facing a bare wall in darkness. When she is encouraged to turn around ... the audience is expecting – and gets – a shock!

There is perhaps an unintentional sense of sadness in the conclusion to the story. While it's true that the odd-numbered Assignments have more whimsical, less compromised endings, it's difficult not to feel a little sorry for Rob. After spending six episodes trying to get his parents back, when they are returned, both are dismissive and snap at him to get on with his homework while giving all their attention to having fun with Helen. An appreciative smile plays on Rob's lips, but as he leaves Helen's room and descends the stairway, he mentally hears Sapphire's goodbye. He looks forlorn for a moment, and then carries on walking downstairs, his footsteps heavier this time. Sapphire's voice seems to stir a reaction in him that he's far from being a man, but also no longer a boy. And with the departure of the agents – people who have been his companions for at least three days – he's once more alone, only now he's more aware of his isolation. It's an oddly touching moment in a scary but generally upbeat serial.

ASSIGNMENT TWO

EPISODE	UK TRANSMISSION	TIME	DURATION	AUDIENCE SHARE
ONE	Tue: 31 Jul 1979	19:00	27′01m	22%
TWO	Thur: 2 Aug 1979	19:00	25′40m	21%
THREE @	Tue: 7 Aug 1979	19:00	24′50m	18%
FOUR @	Thur: 9 Aug 1979	19:00	25′33m	20%
ONE *	Tue: 30 Oct 1979	19:00	27′01m	19%
TWO *	Thur: 1 Nov 1979	19:00	25′40m	20%
THREE *	Tue: 6 Nov 1979	19:00	24′50m	19%
FOUR *	Thur: 8 Nov 1979	19:00	25′33m	20%
FIVE	Tue: 13 Nov 1979	19:00	25′40m	22%
SIX	Thur: 15 Nov 1979	19:00	26′34m	20%
SEVEN	Tue: 20 Nov 1979	19:00	26′08m	22%
EIGHT	Thur: 22 Nov 1979	19:00	25′49m	20%

* The first four episodes were repeated as part of the initial run, hence their inclusion here. See *Mission Brief* for further details.
@ Parts 3 and 4 were not broadcast on these dates in the Thames, Southern, HTV or Ulster areas.

GUEST CAST:
Gerald James (Tully), Tom Kelly (Soldier/Pearce), David Woodcock (1st Voice/1st Submariner), David Cann (2nd Voice/Pilot), and several uncredited extras.

TECHNICAL PERSONNEL:
Maureen Riscoe (Casting), Mary Gibson (Costumes), Len Penfold (Sound, episodes 2-5), Henry Bird (Sound, episodes 1 & 6), Bob Woodhouse (Sound , episodes 7 & 8), Mike Whitcutt (Cameras), Neil Guy (Vision Mixer), John Crane (Vision Control, episodes 1-7), Mary Forrest (Vision Control, episode 8), John Hawkins (VTR Editor), Mary Southgate (Make-Up), Ann Murphy (Stage Manager), Ivor Weir (Title Sequence), Cyril Ornadel (Music), Jim Boyers (Lighting), Shaun O'Farrell (Floor Manager, episodes 1-6), Pete Wernham (Floor Manager), Jeremy Van Bunnens (Floor Manager, episodes 7 & 8), Joyce Lewsey (Production Assistant, episodes 5, 6, & 8), Sonia Hampson (Production Assistant, episodes 1 & 2), Glenys Collins (Production Assistant, episodes 3, 4 & 7), Shaun O'Riordan/David Foster (Directors), Stanley Mills (Designer), David Reid (Executive Producer), P J Hammond (Creator/Writer) and Shaun O'Riordan (Producer). An ATV Network Production.

SYNOPSIS:
George Tully spends his evenings trying to contact the dead at Dewerton Station, an abandoned and unused railway halt that is rumoured to be haunted. After two months, in late October, he finds himself joined by Sapphire and Steel, who are concerned that supernatural activity in the station is increasing. Together they discover that the spirit of a soldier killed after the First World War ceasefire has been brought to Dewerton. The soldier, Private Sam Pearce, is joined by an increasing number of spirits, including a dead RAF pilot and a submarine crew, all of whom harbour resentment over their untimely deaths. The creature controlling them is a mass of darkness, feeding off their resentment and bitterness in order to grow. Negotiations with both the spirits and the creature prove unsuccessful, as the powerful entity threatens to take Sapphire's face and eyes in revenge for their interference, and places Steel in suspended animation, pushing him forwards in time. Unable to find any other way to resolve the situation with such a powerful enemy, Steel offers the entity the life of George Tully, four years before he is expected to die. The entity agrees, releasing the spirits of the undead and leaving the station, knowing that it will have all the resentment it needs from Time in claiming an innocent life.

SAPPHIRE:

Sapphire is shown to do 'spot checks', which determine a person's biological construction by touch. It is hinted that Steel can do this as well, but he moans that it's 'not his territory'. Sapphire later states this more clearly, clarifying, 'You can't exactly do a spot analysis, can you?' – though as this is actually said by Sapphire's *doppelgänger* controlled by the entity, rather than Sapphire herself, it may be unreliable. Another power Sapphire possesses that Steel doesn't is the ability to see microscopic dust particles, as witnessed in the seventh episode. ('I can't see anything.' 'No, but I can.')

Sapphire is also shown to have the power of a medium to speak to spirits, and is described by Steel as an '(Earth) history expert'. As in the first story, it is stated here that her power to take time back can hold time for a day; she manages 22.736 hours in this particular story. Further hints are given about her and Steel's telepathic abilities, with George Tully questioning, 'Some method of thought transference, is it?' 'Something like that, yes,' Sapphire replies.

OLD BLUE EYES IS BACK:

Sapphire's eyes turn blue five times in the story, now realised as a familiar light blue effect with pulsating sound. However, the most striking variation with her eyes here has to be the full black contact lenses that Lumley wears in the final episode, an uncomfortable but effective image.

'HELP ME, STEEL!'

Although there's a notable shift towards independence, the second story still very much depicts Steel as the experienced operator, and Sapphire as the trainee novice. Sapphire rescues Steel from being transformed into a dead pilot, but her attempts to direct the mission and throw scorn on Steel's methods are constantly ignored, Steel commanding all the way through.

It's also notable that Steel's hand is forced in the mission when Sapphire is directly threatened and attacked by the entity; first by the threat of losing her eyes and her brain, then by it taking her face and leaving a mass of contorted flesh behind.

STEEL:

Although hinted at in the first story, this is the first time that both agents are shown to teleport. This is subtly introduced in the fourth episode, where Steel communicates telepathically with Tully from an adjacent room (showing he is also able to conduct thought projection with humans, though this appears to be a one-way process) then appearing at Tully's left side. A 'zing' sound effect is heard, but the process of movement goes unseen, save for Tully's reaction.

Steel is also shown to be able to stop another's bodily movement, freezing Tully with a touch, an act that is later undone by Sapphire. In the sixth episode we get the first hint that Steel has extraordinary strength to call on. However, it is not clarified whether the wood he snaps with his hands so easily is rotten or not. That said, his snapping of Tully's wires in the first episode without tripping over them, and later being shown to be bulletproof, are both evidence of a man that is more than human. Steel's unusual physiognomy is also raised when he tells Sapphire in the seventh episode, 'I also fell asleep. And I don't sleep!' Not only does this imply that she didn't know, but it also implies that Sapphire *does* sleep, showing a difference in their physical functioning, as well as possibly contradicting events in the first story. The reason it is only possibly a contradiction is that three episodes earlier Steel tells Tully, after being advised to close his eyes, 'I prefer to stay awake, thank you.' This perhaps suggests that Steel's habitual wakened state is by his own choice, and that he is capable of sleep if he wishes.

Steel seems to have such powerful lungs that he can blow out a candle from several feet away, and he doesn't know the words to 'Pack Up Your Troubles'. He quickly learns them from Tully, though, showing he has a keen memory. Steel has also never heard of post-hypnotic states or the subconscious mind.

THE ELEMENTS:

There is a hint in the second episode that Sapphire and Steel are governed by more than one … thing? Bemoaning the constant wars of Earth, Steel says, 'Sometimes I wonder why *they* bother to send us here.'

FUTURE ASSIGNMENTS:
Steel possibly sets events in motion for the agents' personal futures, as his actions in Assignment Two's final episode cause a resentment from Time that could last 'five hundred years, maybe a thousand'. How Time takes revenge for Steel's breaking of the rules could be something he and Sapphire find out at the end of the series …

STRANGE RELATIONSHIP:
During the first episode Sapphire playfully tells Steel about the railway hotel. 'How romantic,' he grimaces. More tellingly, Steel gets repeatedly impatient and evasive with Tully's questioning. 'That young woman, is she a relative of yours or just a friend?' the man asks. 'Business associate,' replies Steel. Tully begins to elaborate about how difficult it is to find a compatible partner, before breaking off and questioning, 'Business associate?' with a disbelieving look on his face. A few minutes later, he again quizzes Steel on the subject, asking if they've been working together long. 'Quite a long time, yes.' Tully asks if their relationship works well. 'Perfect,' snaps Steel, with a tone that clearly warns Tully never to broach the subject again.

In the third episode, Steel places a chaste kiss on Sapphire's hand. Soon after, she tries to reassure an unsettled Steel by placing her hand on his shoulder, and he shrugs it off. In episode seven he plants a kiss on her cheek, and in the last episode they embrace. Perhaps the most significant remark is Steel describing Sapphire as, 'the Sapphire I've grown to know and love' in episode six.

YOU MAY REMEMBER ME FROM …

GERALD JAMES:
James appeared in a number of one off plays and individual episodes of television, as well as in a big screen role as Frazier in the James Bond movie *The Man with the Golden Gun* (1974). The Welsh actor could be seen in episodes of *All Creatures Great and Small* (1978), *Last of the Summer Wine* (1975), *The Professionals* (1978) and two entries in the BBC's *Play for Today* (1975/1977). James also appeared in other genre television productions, including playing Uncle Barnabus in *A Traveller in Time* the year before he appeared in *Sapphire & Steel*. He died in June 2006, aged 88.

DAVID CANN: Cementing *Sapphire & Steel*'s place as a favourite with the thirtysomething generation, David Cann's role as the pilot predated his career as an arch comic actor from the late 1990s on. Appearing in multiple cutting edge comedies (including playing a surreal doctor in 2000's *Jam,* a role he reprised, after a fashion, in episodes of *EastEnders* in 2004), Cann has carved out his own niche in the industry. Other works include *Brass Eye* (1997), *People Like Us* (1999), *Black Books* (2000), *Beast* (2001) and *Saxondale* (2006).

A RADA educated actor with an extensive theatre background, Cann also appeared in a number of straight roles, including as Mr Bentley in eight episodes of *Grange Hill* during the early '90s, and as an Incident Commander in *Silent Witness* (1999). In 2007 he took part in an experiment for Wysiwyg Films, attempting to make an 80 minute feature film in 80 hours. The resulting movie - *Dead Eyes* - was released in September of that year. Other recent roles have included *Run, Fatboy, Run* (2007) and a solicitor in *Two Pints of Lager and a Packet of Crisps* (2009).

TOM KELLY:
Kelly is probably most famous to genre fans as Nova in the second episode of *Blake's 7,* 'Space Fall' (1978), or as one of the Vardans in the *Doctor Who* serial 'The Invasion of Time' (1978). Kelly had earlier appeared in *Doctor Who* as a guard in 'The Sun Makers' (1977), and has since been in episodes of *Agony* (1981), *Shine On Harvey Moon* (1984) and *Dempsey and Makepeace* (1985).

DAVID FOSTER:
Foster had worked in genre television before, having directed four episodes of the *Timeslip* serial 'The Day Of The Clone' (1971). Other television work included the children's comedy series *Your Mother Wouldn't Like It* (1985-1988), *Tightrope* (1972) and *Them And Us* (1985), a six-part drama that featured David Collings. Foster was also the producer of youth programmes *Y.E.S.* (1987), *Murphy's Mob* (1982-1985) and *Four Idle Hands* (1976).

MISSION BRIEF:
With the increased workload on both this serial and prepping the following two stories, Shaun O'Riordan brought in David Foster to direct the 'upstairs' sequences. Foster had known O'Riordan for

over 20 years when the story came to be made, having been senior cameraman on *The Larkins* (ITV, 1958-1964) while O'Riordan acted in the series. Foster recalled that, 'Shaun's technical experience, as an actor, while adventurous, was limited. When he was asked to do *Sapphire & Steel* he remembered that I had directed *Timeslip*, another series involving puzzles with time, and that I had devised some technical effects. He told me about the effects he would need to do, and I offered a few ideas, so it was natural that when the first story became a series he should ask me to join him as co-director.'

Production dates on all six stories went uncharted. However, David Cann, the actor playing the ghost pilot, remembered: 'There was a strike while we were shooting. The electricians stopped work. This was in 1978 (I think), a year before the "winter of discontent", and the unions were all-powerful then. Our contracts expired and we had to be re-hired when work resumed.' Design plans for some of the scenery list 9-10 March 1979 as VTR dates for a portion of the taping.

An ITV strike disrupted broadcast of many programmes, including this serial. After the screening of the first four episodes, the series was discontinued in August 1979, with the entire serial being shown from the beginning in October.

The scene where Sapphire's eyes turn black was Joanna Lumley's least favourite part of the series, requiring anesthetic in her eyes in order to stop her involuntarily crying in pain. Despite the discomfort of the plastic coverings, the end result was well received, David Cann observing: 'The most dramatic of special effects were the "black eyes" Joanna wore for one episode. They were like over-sized contact lenses and looked really scary!'

The verse of *The Bible* that Tully quotes in episode two is from 'Revelations' 14:13, while the prayer he chants in episode six is a general prayer known as 'A Collect For Aid Against Perils'.

The song 'Pack Up Your Troubles' was written in 1915 by George and Felix Powell, with George writing under the pseudonym 'George Asaf'. Not including reprises over episodes, a truncated version gets sung a total of seven times, and whistled 16. Also whistled by Sam Pearce in the sixth episode is the 1912 song 'It's A Long Way To Tipperary' by Jack Judge and Harry Williams.

The song Sapphire sings while under a trance as Eleanor is 'Tom Tiddler's Ground', referring to an old children's game not dissimilar to the modern 'tag'. The phrase appears in the serialised thirty-fourth chapter of Charles Dickens's *Nicholas Nickleby* (1839) and is also the title of a short story (1861) by the same author. In 1989 P J Hammond wrote an episode of *The Bill* with this as the title, which aired on 22 June.

David McCallum's strong involvement in the creative process led to two notable elements of design on this story. He suggested placing white paper on the 'tunnel' to create a sense of depth and perspective, the white paper on screen appearing to be the tunnel's mouth. Also, he suggested that his character spend the story wearing a dinner jacket.

At just over 27 minutes, the first episode is the longest of the entire series.

GOOFS:

A goof occurs four minutes into episode two when Tully struggles with a locked door - the wall wobbles and not the door.

In the same episode, David McCallum drops an Americanism into Steel's usually mannered speech patterns when he says of Tully, 'I'm gonna send him home.'

Finally, while not a 'goof' as such, Mr Tully's third candle at the very start of the story does seem to produce rather more illumination than would be strictly natural ...

THE CLIFFHANGERS:

- EPISODE ONE: Steel urges Sapphire to leave the station platform as she is taken over by the form of a woman from the Great War and the sound of a marching band is heard in the distance ...
- EPISODE TWO: Steel faces death as he becomes overtaken by the spirit of a pilot in a crashing plane.
- EPISODE THREE: Steel steps forward to rescue Tully and Sapphire, his clothes changing form as he does so. Behind him, Sam Pearce appears and watches on malevolently.
- EPISODE FOUR: In a trance, Sapphire takes on the persona of someone who is known to Sam. As the contact is made, Sapphire cries in pain and Sam shouts out in horror.
- EPISODE FIVE: As Tully watches over Sapphire's motionless body, the sound of Sam whistling 'Pack Up Your

Troubles' can be heard.

- EPISODE SIX: Steel wakes to find himself trapped in barbed wire and being taunted by Sam.
- EPISODE SEVEN: Sapphire summons the entity for a final negotiation ...

OVERVIEW:
Sapphire & Steel's finest hour, the second story deals with regret, loss and bitterness.

Like the opening story, it primarily succeeds by being so openly terrifying. Here, though, with Hammond fully aware of the later timeslot the series has garnered, the horror becomes focused onto more adult concerns. Consequently, for a young audience scared out of their wits by the first story's nursery rhymes conjuring up the undead to stalk their house and take away their parents, the second story is almost a welcome respite by comparison. A station platform lined with the dead, with zombie-like hands reaching out to grab Steel as he walks down a flight of stairs; and Sapphire's face distorted with blackened eyeballs and transformed into pulverised flesh. All deeply unsettling images, to say nothing of the chattering voices of the entity itself; an insidious, creeping menace that is seemingly ever-present at the corners of the screen.

Like the majority of *Sapphire & Steel*, the story is slow-moving by modern standards, with a ghost that doesn't even appear in the first episode and long drawn out stretches of dialogue-free sequences. Adding to the quality of the episodes are a superb railway station set (which utilises the raised platforms to present some superb low angle shots), lighting so subtle that the darkness of the entity becomes a very real and tangible threat, and Cyril Ornadel's moody, haunted and mournful score. The whole thing is once again extremely theatrical, with varied eulogies that would work as well on stage as on screen, and actors walking in and out of shot with a purposefully static, European style camerawork. In particular, Tom Kelly delivering a lengthy soliloquy on the pasque flower is the kind of storytelling that could easily be reproduced in the theatre. Of the theatricality, co-director David Foster declared that it wasn't a conscious aim: 'We decided from the start that we did not want it to be "science fiction with Men in Silver Suits," just a natural world in which time had been put out of joint. For that, the more normal the shooting, the stranger the time distortions would appear. As most directors do, I think we just used a style that suited the action. Some of the walking out of shot would be because the sets filled the studio several times over, and the walk out of shot would give us the excuse to cut to them coming into the next set, a week later. We had our own games with time, too!'

Although the budget was adequate for the time, there's a homespun charm to proceedings, be it Sapphire's budget-saving observation, 'There are two more floors like this' in the first episode, or the numerous occasions where lighting and sound effects are used to substitute for shifts in time. Never did *Sapphire & Steel* feel so much like a stage production as this, and it's a charming, almost surreal quaintness. Even the necessary special effects have a level of opportunistic zeal, with shots of black and white illustrations to capture the imagery of the Great War in episode three. The same sequence sees a hand with a missing finger covered in blood – actually the hand of a studio worker whom Shaun O'Riordan approached and asked if he could photograph. Neil Guy, the vision mixer on the first two stories, recalled of the creeping Darkness itself: 'It was a piece of artwork on a caption board, which was processed through the mixer and superimposed on the required background. Its movement was supplied by the cameraman moving it through frame manually as required. No computer assisted effects to do this sort of thing existed then.' The second episode in particular contains the bulk of such practices, almost feeling like a work of surrealist cinema as Lumley reacts to a blue background and having her hair blown by a wind machine, and the cliffhanger features McCallum in flying goggles revolving around the screen. David Cann, the actor bringing the ghost pilot to life, said of the special effects: 'They were pretty primitive compared to the computerised extravagances one sees today. I vaguely remember lip-synching the dialogue with David McCallum on the studio floor more or less as the scenes were recorded. Quick and simple.'

Although there was reportedly a relaxed atmosphere on set, the production was beset with strike action and saw last-minute creative decisions being made, as Cann explained: 'The script for the final episode was delivered late and we were all wondering how the plot would be resolved. We went into the studio with only a vague idea of what we were doing. The cameraman had to strap a lamp onto the top of the camera so that wherever he pointed it was lit, there having been no time to work out a lighting scheme.' Another situation saw the show's headlining star take a directorial decision in order to satisfy needs: 'One episode was over-running in rehearsal and some trimming was needed. David [McCallum] said, "No problem. Just cut all the entrances and exits. We don't need to see people coming in and going out. There's nothing useful in watching doors open and close."'

In terms of the story itself, we see another neat narrative twist by Hammond, wherein the secondary plot (what would be known in today's terms as the 'B plot') becomes the primary focus, and the 'A plot' the backdrop to events. Taking that secondary plot first, we find the story populated by Tom Kelly's sensitive portrayal of a dead soldier, Sam Pearce. Simmering with both hurt and resentment, Kelly remains sympathetic whether conspiring to trap Steel or pining for an unrequited love. Though Pearce is the driving force, the element that all three main characters are there to investigate, he's rarely seen in the same scene with any of them, instead remaining on the periphery. Not only does the relationship between the agents and ghost hunter George Tully become the meat of the story, but it's also the unexpected resolution of Tully's character arc that takes precedence over Pearce's.

The age difference between Pearce and his teacher Eleanor (12 years, incidentally the same age difference as between McCallum and Lumley) can only engender further sympathy for Pearce, and give the impression of a besotted schoolboy taken advantage of by someone in a duty of care. Though the relationship between Pearce and his teacher took place after he'd left school and was an adult, the betrayal of psychological trust is still glaring. Pearce leads a procession of embittered ghosts taken before their time, but the curious man-child persona he possesses means his hold over them is tenuous, and his fear of the Darkness itself palpable. While the two time agents plot to send him back to where he came, he hides in darkened corners, crying, and pleading with the Darkness for help.

With Pearce absent (save for a reprise) in the seventh episode, when he returns for the climax it's with the underpinning of the character in full bloom: a frightened, insecure youth, bitter but terrified. It's here that in order for Pearce to accept that the

Darkness cannot grant him life, Steel defers to his partner with a 'Tell him, Sapphire.' Throughout the story, Sapphire has taken on the personality and form of Pearce's lost love, and been emotionally connected to his pain, even becoming Eleanor and walking arm in arm with the soldier at one point. Thus it's only natural that the romanticised, vulnerable side of Pearce's nature would come to the forefront when confronted by her for the climax. It's perhaps fitting that Pearce's final action in the story is shown not with him on screen, but with basketfuls of flowers left for Sapphire, even though his walking through her in the second episode was a metaphorical rape. Pearce's final scene also has a nice symmetry with one in the fourth episode, where Steel says to him, 'Shake my hand ... or come and sit down with me. Come on, talk with me.' The cliffhanger two episodes later sees Pearce entrap Steel, noting, 'You asked me to sit and talk with you. Well I've sat. And I've talked. On my terms for a change and not yours.' Meanwhile, Pearce's decision to return to non-existence is agreed with a handshake between them. Like the later resolution with Tully, the notion of a handshake removing the spirits of the dead is a very traditionally 'English' response to such tragedy. Though Hammond was once again writing the script episodically with no fixed concept of where the story would lead, such cleverly contained touches and the outstanding climax mean that Assignment Two never actually feels anything but tightly pre-planned.

Considering the political climate in 1979, the serial is quite daring in its dismissal of war as anything noble. Although Sam Pearce's war was the Great War, the imagery of World War Two was still prominent in 1979, and the conflict in Vietnam had ended only four years previously. In the second episode, Sapphire talks of the women at railway stations who 'once cheered [the soldiers] on their way, and made them think that they were heroes.' Steel's response is a sardonic, dismissive smile. Today, when mockery of political leaders and policies is *de rigueur*, it's easy to forget how unusual this was 30 years ago. Steel even steps up such open criticism with his line bemoaning 'great wars ... civil wars ... holy wars ... I sometimes wonder why they bother to send us here.'

One interesting element is how the description of ghosts has shifted since the first Assignment. While there they were 'visual refractions', here it's fully established that we're dealing with the dead. Although they are referred to as 'after images', Steel leaves the viewer in no doubt during his first blunt exchange with Pearce: 'Who were you?' 'Who am I, more like?' 'No. Sorry, but you're dead.' We even receive a form of explanation as to how this can take place, Sapphire informing Tully: 'The persona lives on [...] in the atmosphere ... It only has to be activated.' The most curious remark about the nature not only of ghosts, but also of Steel, occurs when Steel has seen the image of three civilian workers calling to him on a submarine: asking Sapphire if they were real living people, he gets the reply, 'Well it could hardly have been as living people, unless of course you were a ghost in their time.' 'I wasn't', comes Steel's cryptic reply. Coincidentally, Lumley would later claim to have been haunted by the ghost of a soldier killed in 1917 France and his lover, while researching a book on wartime romances. In her 2004 autobiography *No Room For Secrets*, she recalled that she was aware of the spirits of the lovers standing behind her as she researched their story, 'resonances' that would stay with her until her work was complete.

The other interesting element of the story's spiritual side is that it is something Sapphire and particularly Steel are not familiar with, and beyond their control. The séance, first popularised by the Spiritualist movement in the mid-1800s, is something Steel alternately distrusts and requires, briefly submitting to Tully's greater experience before once more verbally attacking him when the séance is over. He is sufficiently aware of the practice to suggest, 'Sapphire would make a very good medium,' but later confesses to not knowing what an auto-hypnotic state or the subconscious is. Although this is a very clever trick on the writer's part in order to enable exposition, it also makes the character more satisfyingly flawed and vulnerable than in the first story, a shift that will continue throughout the series. Indeed, the resolution is initiated because Steel is out of his depth, and with Sapphire continually under threat from the Darkness – both being possessed by it and having it take her face – he has run out of options.

The subtle interplay and mild – never overt – hints at sexual attraction also add much to a screenplay replete with subtext. One of the finest readings between the two leads comes with their shared conversation when Lumley is portraying the 'fake' Sapphire, created by the Darkness. Lumley's clipped, almost sardonic, 'Thank you, Steel. Thank you very much,' is a particular highlight, showing the Darkness's belief of what her own personal resentments would sound like. There's also a discernable shift in their relationship since the first story. Sapphire is now very much an equal, even a potential romantic partner, and they share two kisses. This is very much at odds with her 'novice' status in the first Assignment, where she would yield to Steel's dominance. Although Steel still takes command, she argues with his decisions throughout, and his relative failure in the mission further shifts the hierarchy. Their second scene together has Sapphire amused by Steel's terse rudeness (him talking over the top of her) and him not comprehending, or caring, why she should be amused. Steel's sardonic wit is also much increased for this second outing, with him responding to Sapphire's observation that the Darkness hasn't taken up residence in any of the rooms with, 'You expect it to arrive with a suitcase, do you?'

The presence of a more fantastical edge to the story is also notable, though hidden well within the bleakness of the surroundings. Here the power of teleportation is revealed for the first time (something that rather makes a mockery of Lead opening the door forcibly in the prior story, unless it's another power he does not share with his fellow agents), although only Steel is shown to use it – except perhaps at the very ethereal conclusion, when we see Sapphire too fade away from the railway station.[2] A more modern aspect of scientific speculation than telepathy, teleportation's roots in literature can nevertheless be traced back to 1709 with the translation of *Aladdin* and its djinns, or genies (a type of creature also referenced in the fourth Assignment). However, probably the earliest story involving teleporting human beings is Edward Page Mitchell's 1877 work *The Man Without a Body*. The actual word 'teleportation' is widely claimed to have been coined by Charles Fort in his 1931 book *Lo!*.

The most prominent aspect of such tales was the use of machinery in order to achieve the transfer of matter from once place to another. Even television science fiction followed suit, with, of

---

[2] Arguably it is heavily suggested in the first story that all three agents faded away at the end, with Sapphire's goodbye to Rob left hanging telepathically in the air.

course, the TARDIS in *Doctor Who* and, most famously, transporters in *Star Trek*. One of the few entries in either medium to depict teleportation via natural means was the children's television series *The Tomorrow People* (1973-1979), although Alfred Bester also explored the concept in his 1956 novel *Tiger! Tiger!* (known in America as *The Stars My Destination*). Indeed, while *Sapphire & Steel* may not have been a pioneer in the television representation of teleportation it still makes good use of the concept, as the *homo superior* self-styled Tomorrow People of the earlier series used mechanical devices and computer assistance to hone their abilities, whereas with the two time agents the entire process appears to be innate. That the power is never made ostentatious in *Sapphire & Steel*, or even used to aid the plot, is to the series' immense credit. The power of teleportation in *Tiger! Tiger!* – or 'jaunting' as it is dubbed there, after the novel's fictitious founding scientist – relies upon the 'jaunter' knowing the co-ordinates of the place where he or she has to arrive. The term 'jaunting', and this co-ordinate limitation is also used in *The Tomorrow People*. This allows for many interesting dilemmas to befall the characters in the book and series, such as being imprisoned and so on, but would, if applied to *Sapphire & Steel*, give a rational explanation as to why the agents teleport only to places they know the location of, or have visited before. A popular wish fulfillment power, the concept of teleportation, along with time manipulation, was brought back to mainstream audiences in 2006 with the character Hiro Nakamura in the popular NBC series *Heroes*, and was the sole focus of *Jumper*, one of 2008's major motion pictures.

Frightening and moving in equal measure, the second story owes its success partly to the chemistry between the two leads, but partly also to the presence of a bold guest star in Gerald James as Tully. Although the character is there initially to act as an aide to the two agents and a backdrop to the story of the soldier, his role actually inverts as the story progresses, with him becoming the primary focus. One appealing aspect about the serial is that it presents in Tully a positive portrayal of a Christian, something rare in television, particularly in modern terms. This may also suggest that Assignment Two revolves around the theme of faith. Tully's belief in the good of humanity is what compels him to contact the dead from the outset, and throughout the story he undergoes a crisis of faith. After being terrified of the Darkness and leaving Sapphire and Steel behind (his 'I'll get help' quickly changing to 'I'll send back help' after he is almost driven insane by fear), he confesses to Steel that he has lost all belief, and likens dealing with the Darkness to dealing with the Devil. It's an interesting moment in that it allows the character to show a flawed side to his previously likeable nature, rendering him even more three dimensional, and also allows the two agents to resume their roles as heroic icons, in that they are the ones able to face the Darkness. With the subtext of religious belief, it's perhaps not a coincidence that the flower Sam Pearce picks for Eleanor is the pasque flower, the name of which references the Jewish Passover, as the flower blooms, as in the story, at Eastertime.

Yet even in respect of faith, Hammond presents a suitably bleak, black-humoured twist to events. Perhaps the most overt reference to religion occurs in the sixth episode, where Steel is surrounded by darkness, ready to be consumed. The shot cuts to Tully reciting a prayer, immediately after which a white door appears through the darkness to release Steel. The twist being that the door to his salvation leads to him being enmeshed in barbed wire and placed in suspended animation. Hammond's own recollection of such scenes seems to confirm that this particular instance wasn't intended: 'There were a few religious undertones in story two. I suppose they couldn't be avoided when doing a show about the "resurrection" of the dead. And Gerald James's almost unconscious ad-lib of, "Though I walk through the valley of the shadow of death," was certainly one of them. But I don't recall any planned references regarding the white doors. Could have been the director's whim.'

The other major nod to religion is that Steel uses Tully's crucifix to offer his life to the Darkness, and gives Tully back his faith when he is sold. There's also a delightful ambiguity in Tully's actions when sacrificed. We already know he's an astute man – he picks up on the thought transference between Sapphire and Steel after just one episode – and it's suggested that he knows he's to be killed. Waving goodbye to Steel and taking determined steps forward, it's as if he is aware that he is giving his life to spare the lives of the others, making his own personal offering in the spirit of the Christ he follows. Although we learn in the first episode that

Tully's life expectancy is just over four years, a poignancy is still added when he muses to Sapphire in the sixth episode about his hopes for a brighter future: 'I'm looking forward to reaching 70 … even getting into my eighties, if it means I should find success.' However, in giving himself for the good of others, Tully has found a way of achieving the peace he tells them he craves.

Perhaps the most daring game Hammond plays with accepted convention is in having his major hero so fundamentally flawed, goading and provoking the likeable Pearce throughout. Though Steel is allowed to display more humour in his reactions than in the first Assignment, those improvisational points lend further sympathy to those he mocks. The refrain of 'Pack Up Your Troubles' is placed in the narrative solely to evoke the sympathetic, romantic character of the soldier, causing Steel to appear callous. The agent's physical bullying of the older Tully is also of note, and it's amusing to see that even the spirit of Eleanor dislikes and distrusts him. It's to David McCallum's immense credit as an actor that he manages to portray such a character without completely alienating the audience.

Such concerns are given to viewers from the outset, challenging their expectations. The series of extended long takes that make up Tully's four-and-a-half minutes in the Booking Hall pre-credits sequence for episode one (utilising fewer than 20 edits) means we spend time with a guest character rather than the stars. Before the credits, Steel's footsteps are heard, the implication being that Steel is the spirit that Tully is attempting to contact, his nerves already jarred by an unexpected flapping pigeon. With the opening titles giving the audience time to dwell on such implications, we return to the narrative to find Steel's back to us, his head out of the top of the frame. Tully, meanwhile, remains the only thing illuminated, a high angle not only putting us almost within Steel's perspective, but also making Tully further emasculated and ineffectual. That our identification point for over six minutes is now violated – his candle forcibly blown out, his neatly prepared string experiment brusquely destroyed – denotes just the beginning of Steel's bullying of the older man, a series of events that culminates in the ultimate betrayal.

We're led to believe that Steel undergoes a change of heart and a softening towards Tully throughout the eight episodes, yet the one thing that most solidifies the story as such an exceptional piece of television is the tragic conclusion. Highly unusual in any genre, here the hero kills the loveable Tully because he can find no other way out of the situation. Though such events do mirror Hammond's own experiences with writing the story (in that he remembered when writing the final episodes Sapphire's earlier statement that Tully's total life expectancy was '57.03 years'), it lacks the feel of artifice, and instead has the audience waiting – in vain – for a last minute reversal of events. Shocking to many on first viewing, the second story has no reprieves, and makes no compromises.

There are isolated moments of genuine humour in the script, largely with the McCallum-James interplay, such as Steel's reaction towards Tully conducting a séance by himself, holding his own hands, or having a one-eyed cat called Nelson. McCallum's take on the character is far more expansive in the larger set, the greatest of the series' studio creations, and quirky touches are added, such as his having a conversation with Tully conducted while lying down. Hammond puts great dialogue in Steel's mouth, from his musing about third-rate grievances to his response to Tully suggesting that ghosts tried to kill them: 'Not quite: they encouraged us to die.' However, such moments are small pinpricks in a script that is oppressively bleak, the latter information given unwittingly by Tully as Steel tries to discover if he has any dependents before sacrificing him.

The real beauty in such a resolution is the sense of understatement. In contrast to modern television works, which frequently opt for a 'tell not show' approach in dialogue, it's refreshing to find a television programme that credits viewers with the intelligence to comprehend all its nuances. Steel's final world-weary glance after sacrificing Tully is a very old fashioned reaction towards death and loss. Like *Sapphire & Steel* itself, such reactions and levels of understatement perhaps belong to a bygone age in the 21st Century. Yet it's this challenging and heartbreaking conclusion that cements Assignment Two as such a classic piece of television.

SEASON TWO

ASSIGNMENT THREE

EPISODE	UK TRANSMISSION	TIME	DURATION	AUDIENCE SHARE
ONE	Tue: 6 Jan 1981	19:00	24'23m	22%
TWO	Thur: 8 Jan 1981	19:00	24'04m	24%
THREE	Tue: 13 Jan 1981	19:00	24'53m	19%
FOUR	Thur: 15 Jan 1981	19:00	24'15m	20%
FIVE	Tue: 20 Jan 1981	19:00	25'31m	16%
SIX	Thur: 22 Jan 1981	19:00	25'55m	21%

GUEST CAST:
David Collings (Silver), Catherine Hall (Rothwyn), David Gant (Eldred), Russell Wootton (Changeling), Adrian Wootton (Younger Changeling, uncredited), Terence Wootton (Youngest Changeling, uncredited) and six uncredited extras.

TECHNICAL PERSONNEL:
Maureen Riscoe (Casting), Mike Whitcutt (Cameras), John Willment (Vision Control), Mary Southgate (Make-Up), Mary Gibson (Costumes), Ron Brown (Programme Administrator), Ann Murphy & Denise Shaw-Vance (Stage Managers), Ivor Weir (Title Sequence), Cyril Ornadel (Music), Jim Boyers (Lighting), Chic Anstiss (Film Cameraman), Glen Cardno (Film Editor), Henry Bird (Sound), Moyra Bird (Vision Mixer), John Hawkins (Video Tape Editor), George Leuenberger (Special

Effects), Jeremy Van Bunnens (Floor Manager), Sonia Hampson (Production Assistant), Stanley Mills (Designer), David Reid (Executive Producer), P J Hammond (Creator/Writer) and Shaun O'Riordan (Director/Producer).

SYNOPSIS:
Three survey groups from a future of approximately 3480, where there is a new system of time and calendar, are sent in capsules for examination and observation of the 20th Century. Two of the groups commit suicide in order to avoid a fate that has followed from the future. The third, comprising a man and woman (assuming the names 'Eldred' and 'Rothwyn', mistakenly believing these to be contemporary) and their baby son, occupy an invisible penthouse flat, their mission titled 'Experimental Project ES/5/777: Urban Examination and Observation'. On the twenty-fifth day of their mission, they stop receiving supplies of nutrition from the future, and psychic and physical attacks begin to occur. Sent to investigate the disturbances are Sapphire and Steel, who are also repeatedly attacked, Sapphire being absorbed into the time crystal powering the heart of the experiment. A third agent, Silver, arrives to aid them, and together they discover that the experiments are powered by a hybrid animal foetus from a future where animals no longer exist. Resentful of the way its kind have been treated, it continues to attack the occupants of the flat, transforming the baby into a grown man capable of sending objects and people forward into the future or back into the past by touch alone. Steel eventually restores the man back into an infant by placing its hands together, then prevents the time travellers from bringing any further chaos into the present by enticing the creature back into the time capsule's workings and sending the capsule back into the future.

SAPPHIRE:
Sapphire appears to have the ability to project music, or the memory of music, in the fifth episode. She is also able to remove herself from time in order to prevent bodily harm - she is strangled by Steel in the final episode, but her healthy voice can be heard while her prone body lies behind him.

OLD BLUE EYES IS BACK:
Sapphire's time manipulation powers cause her eyes to glow dark blue and indigo in this story, not medium blue. While there are no fictional reasons for this, the real behind-the-scenes reason was so that the effect would match the different contact lenses Joanna Lumley needed for the exterior location work on film; the electronic chromakey system could be used only on video.

'HELP ME, STEEL!':
Sapphire spends the third episode dispersed within the time field, only to re-emerge within the rural study group. A similar fate befalls Silver, who spends the fifth episode in a state of non-existence after being touched by the grown baby.

STEEL:
Although Steel having supernatural strength was alluded to in the second story, with him breaking wood with his hands, here it's depicted outright for the first time. In the second and sixth episodes, he is shown hauling an elevator up its shaft and bending its cables with his bare hands. He could kill the grown baby with a blow to the back of the head (episode five), and he also breaks and burns out the elevator's workings in the third episode with a single frustrated blow to the control panel. This previously unseen strength is also used in an attempt to intimidate Silver on more than one occasion, yet the grown child is able to resist and even overpower Steel. Whether this ability of Steel's is a power he has to summon - like Sapphire's 'taking time back' - or whether it's innate is not specified.

On the subject of powers, there's also the mild suggestion that the agents are not fully aware of each other's full capabilities. When Sapphire asks Steel if he's thinking what she's thinking (episode five) his immediate response is 'Yes, the same thoughts.' While this could possibly be a throwaway remark or an attempt to illustrate that they've developed empathy, it also seems to imply that Steel is aware of Sapphire's state of mind without her having to use thought projection. The counterpart of this is that Steel doesn't appear exactly aware of how Sapphire's time reversal abilities work - or that possibly they've been uniquely accelerated by the creature within the capsule. When she tells Steel that she only had to think of time rolling back for it to happen his incredulous reply is, 'You only had to *think* it?'

Steel's lack of knowledge when it comes to Earthly matters is again highlighted in episode two when he fails to recognise the creature that attacked him on the rooftop: 'A bird ... some kind of bird.' 'It was a swan,' Sapphire helpfully informs him. Finally, it's implied that a fall from a high rooftop could, quite naturally, kill him.

THE ELEMENTS:

In episode three we are introduced to Silver, played by David Collings. A white male of average build and with red hair, he claims he 'just happened to be passing' before he joined the mission, though Steel suspects he was sent. Throughout the story we learn that he is aware not only of the fate of the inhabitants of the other capsules, but also of the details of Steel's briefing. ('No. Not wrong. Incomplete, perhaps, but not wrong.')

He too can teleport, like Sapphire and Steel, and shares a telepathic link with them. He describes himself as 'a technician', with infallible, built-in 'instant reduplication'. He also fixes a knot Steel placed in a lift's cable, though whether this is by physical strength or not is unascertained. (In fact, the final episode sees the knot back in place, indicating it may have been some trick of time or dimensional displacement - Silver's explanation is, 'I fixed the lift, I'm afraid ... I wasn't going to walk up. It's all right, I haven't touched your knot.')

Silver carries with him a zipped black wallet-like bag with a series of implements inside. With them (and seemingly without them) he has the power to transmute objects, in this case a nail into liquid form, glass powder back into whole glass, a necklace into a handkerchief and a ball bearing into a light bulb. He uses a hollow metal tube as a blow torch and has an unspecified device with the outward appearance of a solar calculator. His main function in the assignment is to use various household items - including a sink plug chain, a ball bearing, a thimble and a coat hook - to engineer a device with which to penetrate the barrier.

Finally, after Silver is attacked by the Changeling, Sapphire rather obliquely claims that Silver has been sent back 'to his beginnings - maybe even further than that.'

STRANGE RELATIONSHIP:
One of the most notable points about Silver is that - unlike Lead - he appears to have been created partially to forge an 'eternal triangle' with the two titular agents. As with Sapphire and Steel's own relationship, any suggestion of romantic involvement is ambiguously alluded to, rather than directly spelt out. It was a part of the character's conception that David Collings was directly involved in, as with many of the more eccentric aspects of Silver: 'I sort of brought that in. I started to flirt with [Sapphire] so there was some sort of back story to it. All the trickery bits, changing screws and things, melting into my hands, I sort of devised all that.'

The third episode sees Steel distressed after Sapphire has disappeared, telling Silver, 'I need Sapphire back.' 'Oh, quite, I know how you feel,' replies Silver, 'We ... well, she's very attractive.' When Sapphire remarks on Silver's beginnings, Steel claims he cannot imagine Silver as a baby, Sapphire the same of Steel. Steel seems affronted and claims to have origins that are positive and impeccable, if 'inexpressible.' Three scenes later Steel is still dwelling on the assertion, defiantly thinking to himself, 'I have *impeccable* origins'. He also appears jealous of Silver's obvious rapport with Sapphire, even 'talking' over him during their three-way telepathic link.

Perhaps the most overt example of this 'chemistry' is when Silver and Steel breach the time barrier to rejoin Sapphire. We see Steel in a vortex, with no indication of how long he's spent in there. When he emerges, Silver is face to face with Sapphire, gazing at her lasciviously with his jacket collar upturned. Steel takes obvious discomfort in their familiar body language, particularly when Sapphire smoothes down Silver's collars for him and carries on talking with her hands on Silver's shoulders.

A sense of appeasement is reached in the fifth episode, Steel placing his hands around Sapphire's shoulders and conceding to admiring the missing Silver, apparently just to please Sapphire. (Though her impassioned, 'I miss him,' does draw an emotional second glance from Steel. This exchange was not in the original camera script for the episode.) In the same episode, Steel fails to break through a wall. 'Silver could do it', says Sapphire. 'Yes, Silver probably could,' he grimaces. Silver, for his part, becomes impatient with Sapphire in the final episode when she places Steel before him, though there is a scene where he and Sapphire, unseen by Steel, briefly hold hands

YOU MAY REMEMBER ME FROM ...

DAVID GANT:
A versatile actor, Gant has appeared in such guises as a KGB Official in *Firefox* (1982), a London *Maitre d'* in *Chaplin* (1992) and Mohamed Aziz in *Wish You Were Here* (2005). Recent roles have included a part in the popular detective television series *Rosemary & Thyme* (2006) and playing Victor in *S Club: Seeing Double* (2003). A recent film role with *Sapphire & Steel*ish overtones saw Gant as a writer fighting two of his own characters who try to change their destiny in *Ink Control* (2006). However, the three most prominent films that Gant has appeared in are *Gandhi* (1982), *Brazil* (1985) and *Braveheart* (1995). Gant also has an extensive theatre background of over 40 productions, including twice playing Lear at the Southwark Playhouse.

RUSSELL WOOTTON:
Wootton could be seen as Marty in the *Star Cops* episode 'Trivial Games and Paranoid Pursuits' (1987). Outside the genre he also appeared in episodes of *Rab C Nesbitt* (1996), *Shoestring* (1980), *Minder* (1984), *Dalziel and Pascoe* (1996), *Sink Or Swim* (1982) and *Don't Wait Up* (1988). An accomplished theatre actor, he spent much of 2007 in tours of *Twelfth Night* and *Macbeth*, with his most recent film role coming the following year in the short *Made By Maggie* (2008).

MISSION BRIEF:
This was the only *Sapphire & Steel* story to use both a location shoot - ATV House, in Great Cumberland Place, London doubled as the tower block - and film stock. While camera angles increased the illusion of danger, David McCallum really *was* walking along the roof's ledge, and no-one involved with the production can recall a safety net or harness being used to protect the actor.

The baby with accelerated growth is credited onscreen as a 'Changeling'. This is a reference to medieval folklore, in which a child would be stolen by trolls or fairies and replaced by a double. Coincidentally, in Scandinavia, which is where most of the stories originated, such creatures were said to be afraid of steel, and parents would often place steel items above a baby's cradle as protection.

The four ages of the Changeling were played by four separate actors. Although only Russell Wootton is credited, his nephews Adrian and Terence were used to play the older and younger versions respectively. The baby itself was actually played by a girl!

As with all the *Sapphire & Steel* stories, no details of production dates have been kept in the archives. However, Russell Wootton recalled, 'I think my story was rehearsed and recorded in about three months - January, February and March of 1980.' Such a period would appear to be corroborated by his nephew, Adrian, who confirmed that the scenes with him and his brother were taped in around an hour on Sunday 24 February 1980. The original designers' plans for the story list 'VTR Dates' as 22-25/1/1980, while the script for the fifth episode (which was written concurrently with production) is date marked '26.02.80'.

From at least this point onwards, David McCallum used to travel back to his family in America each weekend while taping the series, making it a gruelling schedule for the star. David Collings, playing Silver, noted, 'He used to commute from New York to do it. He used to go back to New York every weekend. That was part of his contract.'

The nudity seen in the story was not originally planned, and was improvised by Shaun O'Riordan on the day of the take. Russell Wootton recalled that clever camera angles were scheduled to disguise the fact that he was wearing underwear, but: 'We had a couple of goes at the scene then suddenly Shaun declared that it wasn't working and did I mind taking my pants off? I remember him calling across the studio that it would really be very helpful and that he would ensure that my fee for that episode would be generously increased. Crikey, bum money!'

Discussing how the effect of Sapphire and Steel's 'telepathic' conversations and other overdubbed sounds were achieved, Wootton remembered: 'I'm pretty sure that the telepathic dialogue was pre-recorded and played in "live" during each take. It would have been simpler for them to have something to react to. As far as the other sounds go, I think the time controller sounds were added afterwards, but the baby music thing was set off live and I reacted to it accordingly.'

Renowned stage and film actor Sir Antony Sher was the first choice to play Silver. However, he returned the script unopened, citing *Sapphire & Steel* as the 'nastiest programme' he'd ever seen.

For Assignment Three, commercial breaks were introduced, a practice that continued until the end of the series.[3] As captions signifying 'End Of Part One' and 'Sapphire & Steel Part Two' were placed over the top of the image, this led to lost material and occasional removed lines when the captions were edited out for VHS and early DVD releases. The most notable example of this comes with the fifth episode of Assignment Three, where David McCallum says the line, 'There's a field outside this place ... and now, apparently, a time barrier within' with the 'Part Two' caption over the top.

GOOFS:

The end of the first episode sees a floating pillow moving around the penthouse. While the wires holding the pillow up can't be seen, the stretches they make on the pillow's fabric are only too obvious.

The swan seen in the first and second episodes was an arm-mounted puppet manipulated by uncredited series technician George Douglas. A careful look at the sequence (particularly with use of a pause button) reveals both Douglas's head and white woolly hat in shot. In Douglas's own words, he considered the hat to be ideal both for keeping him warm and for matching the swan's colouring. 'However, Shaun O'Riordan obviously didn't share my opinion, for suddenly, in the middle of filming, he stopped and called out to me, "George, if I see that hat of yours once more in shot, I'm going to knock your bloody head off!"'

The start of the fourth episode has Steel 'communicate telepathically' with Sapphire, using McCallum's prerecorded lines. His line about 'sand, soda ash and vine' is accidentally played in twice.

---

[3] It was standard ITV practice not to have commercial breaks in programmes made primarily for children, which would explain why none were included in the Assignment One episodes.

The eyes of the fully grown Changeling and the medium version are brown in colour, but those of the youngest version are grey-blue.

A goof that goes unnoticed on screen but occurred during recording concerns the very last scene. As David Collings recalled, 'I found this little mouse in the capsule, which peed on my hand.'

THE CLIFFHANGERS:

- EPISODE ONE: Steel is attacked by a creature resembling a swan, an attack that pushes him ever nearer a rooftop edge ...
- EPISODE TWO: Sapphire is absorbed into the time unit, crying out, 'The pain ... the pain ... for always ... forever.'
- EPISODE THREE: Steel asks Sapphire for further information about the second capsule, as Silver prepares to get them inside.
- EPISODE FOUR: Silver confronts the Changeling, which disperses him with a touch.
- EPISODE FIVE: Sapphire and Steel hear the sound of movement behind a door in the penthouse, and cautiously approach ...

Note: The original planned cliffhanger to the fifth episode featured Steel grappling with the Changeling, whose hand reaches out to touch Steel's face. However, this event occurs significantly earlier in the episode, so timing requirements meant the production ran with a more low-key ending.

OVERVIEW:

Traditionally the least popular *Sapphire & Steel* story, Assignment Three nevertheless has much to recommend it and plays interesting games with storytelling conventions.

For the first and only time, writer P J Hammond steers the series away from fantasy and the uncanny and into more familiar science fiction territory. The concept of time breaking in is abandoned in favour of a more straightforward tale of time travel gone awry.

While this is at odds with the series' own self-imposed remit, it also gives us an unusual new slant on the development of the narrative. Beneath all the supernatural trappings, *Sapphire & Steel* is fundamentally a detective series. The Assignment subverts this slightly by allowing the viewer to be privy to events as they unfold, parallel to the agents' investigations. While the ultimate discovery that the capsule is being controlled by animal consciousness is learnt by us at the same time as it is by Sapphire and Steel, many of the other elements are discovered by the agents after the viewer is already aware of them. The most prominent example occurs in the fifth episode, where Sapphire takes time back to observe the presence of Rothwyn, and her reporting to the communication panel ... a full four episodes after the viewer was witness to this act. In the field of television detection, then, story three lies more in the realm of series like *Columbo* or *Cracker*, rather than *Poirot* or, latterly, *Jonathan Creek*: here the mystery is not whodunit, but *why*, and what the reaction of the investigators will be when they uncover it. In a further toying with this convention, Silver is aware of events before the two lead agents are. While we discover at the same time as Sapphire does that the occupants of the two other capsules have committed suicide, it's information already known to an agent who could easily have passed this on, but hasn't ... a point of characterisation to return to later.

Perhaps the most significant aspect of the case is that – as with the second Assignment – it's another that they can't adequately solve. The creature is not defeated, just led back within the capsule's circuitry and sent back into the future. Sapphire's announcement, 'It is their problem [...] They caused it, let them solve it,' presents a form of resolution different from all those in the other Hammond scripts. While the second and fourth Assignments had the agents achieve their means by compromise, and the first had the cleanest, most efficient consequence, this tale sees a figurative 'reset to zero'. Essentially Sapphire and Steel do nothing but send the capsule back to its own time. All the crises they have faced throughout remain a potential danger; there's nothing to stop the creature attacking Eldred and Rothwyn or retransforming the baby back into a Changeling when they return to the 35th Century. While it's the character development, dramatic punctuation and thematic content that make the story what it is, in terms of the framework upon which it is built, Assignment Three has no real forward progression.

A particular item of note is that Rothywn and Eldred take the opposite of traditional gender roles, Rothwyn being the more proactive throughout. In their interactions with the time agents particularly, Rothwyn is the one doing all the communicating, while Eldred uses her as a human shield to hide behind when intimidated by Steel. Hammond claimed, 'Without wishing to sound like some kind of die-hard campaigner, I have always been opposed to discrimination of any kind and was on the side of Women's Lib from the outset. I felt that the Catherine Hall character had every right to be the boss in that story. She was the homemaker, and her information about domestic life and childrearing was more important than her partner's information.' It's a philosophy that runs throughout Hammond's work, with him holding similar views about Sapphire's proactive stance: 'From the start I had made up my mind that she would not be a bimbo or an appendage of Steel, but someone proactive in her own field. The perfect casting helped to portray that.'

One of the more overlooked elements of the relationship between Eldred and Rothwyn is that while they are clearly sleeping partners there is no firm indication that they are married. Indeed, Hammond refers to Eldred as Rothwyn's 'partner', and at no point in the screenplay is he explicitly identified as the baby's father. They use the term 'our child' just once each, which could suggest that Eldred is a substitute father. His particularly detached dismissal, 'I've just seen the child – there's nothing wrong with it,' adding to this impression. While Rothwyn's insistence on calling the baby 'my child' throughout may be just emphasised maternalism, there's no reason to doubt that she is a single mother, with Eldred for support ... a subtle and interesting piece of social commentary from Hammond in 1980.

However, taking this empowerment of Rothwyn to its logical extreme, we can see that she is still presented within the codings of television as 'the vulnerable female'. Professor Elizabeth Ann Kaplan published research into the field of the 'male gaze' in film studies. She and others developed the theory of the objectification of women in the cinematic arts, whereby Western culture projects women through a phallocentric representation, a projection that is not allowed to be returned. While Catherine Hall's character is presented as the dominant partner, she is objectified throughout. One interesting element of the story is that she *is* allowed a hierarchy over the communication panel – we see it from her perspective until over five minutes into the story, and its gradual dominance over her (including the projected images of livestock) is for narrative purposes. Yet one of the first shots of the story is a close up of her bare feet sliding into sandals, while later shots see her change clothes and run her fingers through her hair, accentuating her femininity. Director Shaun O'Riordan admitted to being conscious of this on the commentary of the Region 1 DVD release, describing Hall as 'the most beautiful girl' and making special mention of the fact that he'd got 'a shot of her lovely legs'. (It could be argued that the same thing happens to Lumley – who is dressed in what looks to be a Chinese Katsumushi costume and straight wig throughout – with the first shot of her being her boots, and her first full length mid-shot seeing her head cut off from the camera's field.) Finally, Rothwyn's interaction with the two male agents see her as partially submissive, even allowing Silver (who it is implied has some level of low key telepathic suggestion, not unlike Sapphire in the previous story) to touch her intimately while removing her necklace.

Yet because Eldred and Rothwyn are very much the 'other' in this story (even the villain of the piece, the exploited creature, engenders more sympathy from the viewer than the aloof and ineffectual Eldred) it means the focus is placed upon the agents as those we must empathise with. This does lead to a lightening of the series' tone somewhat, as two anti-heroes who we're not sure we can trust are eventually – by the final story – the victims of time, for whose safety we must be concerned. This broadening of their characters not only sees Steel being portrayed indulging in credibility-threatening feats of strength and an affected musical motif being used to cement Silver's humorous leanings, but also a lessening of the mystery surrounding the characters' origins. The first two stories have us wondering not only where Sapphire and Steel come from, and when, but also who and what they are. Here Hammond's broadening of the comic scope lets us know after 18 episodes that the 'medium atomic weights' were once children. This seems as odds with Steel's earlier suggestion that the swan tried to 'destroy' (not 'kill') him.

The real softening in character comes with Steel. In the previous stories he's been shown as a man with an underdeveloped sense of social skills. His brusque – even downright callous – attitude toward human beings is born not out of a lack of a maturity, but out of a disregard, even a failure to understand why they would require such things as civility and emotional warmth. Here, though, with Silver's open flirting with Sapphire and her free acceptance of such, he becomes openly vulnerable, almost boyishly petulant in response. There are moments, particularly in the fourth episode where Silver and Sapphire are constantly crossing into each other's personal space, where Steel looks lost and openly hurt. It's this transformation from a terse, impatient investigator into an emotionally stunted man of naked affection that drives away the Steel of the previous two adventures.

Although this isn't necessarily a good showcase for David McCallum, with him also having a largely reactive role throughout, he does get to return to his customary abrupt nature in the final instalment. He grips Eldred's face to prove he's 'real', and pushes Rothywn to one side, offering stern words for both of the time travellers. 'Would you have done the same thing?' he asks of them, when it's revealed the members of another capsule sacrificed themselves. 'Because you can always do it now, you know. It would save us a lot of trouble.' Another nice line comes later when Eldred refuses to look in on another survey team's sleeping quarters. 'Are you trying to tell us,' mocks Steel, 'that it's taken fifteen hundred years of troubles, wars and famines … to learn not to peep in one another's bedrooms?'

Acting is strong across the cast. Eldred and Rothwyn are very atypical, left-of-centre characters, but are embodied very well by Hall and Gant. Wootton meanwhile is perfect casting for the unique role of 'baby aged to 30 years'. Speaking of the role, Wootton recalled: 'I don't remember getting a great deal of advice about the character other than being told that he was a man in a baby's body. On set I was often given very specific direction about what I would be feeling or thinking at any given moment. The Changeling (who I think had the name of Bobba) didn't know he was the Changeling. His brain and mind were completely undeveloped, so he reacted mostly on instinct – to cold, kindness, thirst, fear and so on. By sticking to that, I hope it enabled me to behave appropriately, although I had to dig a bit sometimes, because it was a very odd and confusing situation.' It's such a fantastical, extreme role that it contributes towards the serial's lower critical regard. Audiences of the early 1980s weren't perhaps ready to see a naked six foot man in his thirties portraying an overgrown baby, and it was something that Wootton himself was only too aware could easily turn into parody if not pitched correctly: 'I'm aware that I have quite an expressive face, one that could be over expressive for the likes of a TV close-up, so I needed to get the thoughts and feelings right to convey the necessary emotions, rather than mugging, which would have been easy.'

O'Riordan's direction must also be praised, allowing characters to enter rooms in long shot, having the baby emerge as a man behind the reflection of a glass and using a fish eye lens for some of the more surreal aspects. As with the rest of the story, the camera is more mobile and jaunty than before, though the *mise-en-scene* is always foremost in O'Riordan's work. Even the opening shot – the exterior of the tower block, with startled birds in flight not only showing the eerie desolation of the environment but also cleverly mirroring the Assignment's themes – is a considered touch. This is the only one of the six stories to feature film stock, and all of the exteriors are captured on the medium, something Hammond did express slight regret wasn't done for the series as a whole. Although his work as a director did not include the third story ('It was really the luck of the draw; P J Hammond was writing close to production deadlines, and Shaun and I took alternate scripts as they came in'), David Foster was one of the most ardent supporters of the video medium: 'Why should being on video detract? All television is designed to be seen as an electronic picture, so why not shoot it as such. One of the advantages of working on video is that you can see and adjust things as you go along rather than waiting for rushes to come back from the lab. We knew immediately if the effects were working. I think a lot of the special effects would have been much more expensive if they had been done on film, or even impossible. By comparison, film seemed to progress at a snail's pace. The satisfaction of doing an hour and a half of live drama in one transmission is something that is now very rarely experienced.'

This Assignment is *Sapphire & Steel*'s most political story, but the theme of animal cruelty is too forced and contrived to come over really successfully. The final episode sees McCallum deliver an overstated monologue to the sound of seagulls in the background:

'Things that once ran wild, but at least free ... things that breathe ... and ate, and produced their young. Things that swam in the sea. Things that managed to survive - once. Reduced to a few living pieces?' As with the opening episode and its rear projection of abattoirs, or the final episode where the three agents rather stagily turn their backs on the two time travellers, it's somewhat laboured. Hall picking up a leg of lamb to the sound of an overdubbed sheep's cry is also unintentionally amusing. It's perhaps fair to say that *Sapphire & Steel* doesn't quite work as a science fiction series in the fullest sense of the term.

Regulation of vivisection has a long and complex history in Britain, with the Cruel Treatment of Cattle Act being passed by Parliament in 1822, and the SPCA (later the RSPCA) being formed two years later. A law to regulate treatment of animals as a whole dates back to 1876, though it was actually some time after Hammond's story was aired that a revised one was brought into operation, with 1986's Animals (Scientific Procedures) Act. With this in mind, then, while the subtext of vivisection in Assignment Three can be regarded as overstated, it's worth noting that it was a subject rarely tackled on television at the time, particularly in such graphic terms. Although militant action against animal experimentation had occurred in the 1970s (in the most well-publicised case, Ronnie Lee and Cliff Goodman were arrested and sentenced for allegedly taking part in a raid on Oxford Laboratory Animal Colonies in Bicester in 1974), it was during the mid 1980s that animal rights groups began leaning further towards extremist behaviour, a factor that saw tabloid interest rising.

Another highlight of the story is Hammond's fortuitous prediction of reality television. While British science fiction had done this before - most notably in Nigel Kneale's *The Year of the Sex Olympics* (1968) - Hammond's script manages to accurately predict the *Big Brother* format, down to the occupants of the household giving 'diary room' entries in a chair to an unseen observer. However, while extremely provident, we perhaps can't place too much weight on such an ingredient as the satirisation of reality television *wasn't* what Hammond had intended. Yet the portentous elements of the script don't end with the *Big Brother* association. It's also implied that the Earth Eldred and Rothwyn come from is either an entirely enclosed society or the product of global warming, with

Rothwyn recording the observation, 'Our temperatures are normal. That's living inside, of course.' Although this is a direct reference to it being winter, she then notes, 'I'd hate to imagine how we'd survive outside.' A later remark sees her refer to the present as the 'atomic age'.

For the first time, the series also abandons its theatrical roots. Assignment Three is very much a pacier, cliffhanger-led programme for television, the exaggerated spotlight on Catherine Hall in episode two one of the few deviations back to stage melodrama. Yet there's no denying that the story is generally regarded as a bit of a failure on aesthetic levels. Gone are the remote country house and the deserted railway station, and in their place is an apartment decorated in all the glory of 1970s style. Mushroom lampshades meet beige wallpaper, as Eldred tries to emote while wearing a brown shirt and a tanktop. While these elements are there to show Eldred and Rothwyn blending in with their contemporary surroundings, they do date the story more than the relatively 'timeless' settings of the story's peers. With a plastic synthetic animal on the loose and Russell Wootton looking for all the world like a bewildered Leo Sayer, Cyril Ornadel's music seems to follow suit, being at its most intrusive and eccentric. Wootton noted the fashion implications, citing 'the end of an awful perm that was fashionable then' and recalling, 'I remember mucking up the scene where I had touched a big leather sofa with my "offending hand". I touched the sofa and had to immediately stay perfectly still while the sofa was removed and replaced with something resembling its past molecular state. This was fine until what I can only describe as an enormous turd was placed before me. I corpsed and ruined the take.'

This is the point at which *Sapphire & Steel* begins to abandon the format of dark ghost stories and phases in brighter sets and intentional surrealism. While the second aspect would produce some memorable results – such as the chess sets in the final tale, or the Magritte influences in Assignment Four – here those elements stretch only to a pillow making a clucking noise or a cushion creeping up stealthily upon its intended victim. The suggestion of danger from everyday objects is a potentially great one, and Catherine Hall does enable the drama to convey an amount of psychological terror, but frequently the ability to realise these things successfully on screen is beyond the series' budget.

What gives the story its bite is that, while the presentation might be overambitious, it's the most daring in terms of content. While it's all too easy to snigger at David McCallum having to share the screen with a puppet swan or a killer fur coat, this is a television drama that includes a woman fighting the urge to smother her partner and child with a pillow, shows victims of child suicide onscreen and features rear male nudity. The final episode has McCallum, under the control of illusions, strangle Sapphire and just manage to prevent himself from stabbing a baby with a kitchen knife. Easy, 'safe' television this wasn't. P J Hammond observed about his third set of scripts: 'I wasn't deliberately attempting to be daring or different. It was an entity and not a person that was all set to commit infanticide, and semi-nudity had to be part of the parcel with that particular story. And although today's television climate can sometimes be affected by panicky politically correct thinking, I don't think *Sapphire & Steel* had overstepped any boundaries.' Russell Wootton's mixed take on the finished product was: 'Overall I thought it was quite good, I suppose; making an effort to push some boundaries ... I didn't feel it was particularly successful as far as some of the special effects went, which weren't always that convincing, although I thought some of the props were excellent. Perhaps some of the failings were part of its charm. You *could* "see the join", but then some of today's CGIs are just too good.'

While story three has a faster pace than its predecessors, it could be argued that it's still overlong, particularly with a fifth episode that contains almost no narrative progression whatsoever. However, the six instalments are enlivened by David Collings' first appearance as the waspish Silver. His clashes with Steel and his presence in the dynamic - there are several allusions to the effect that he's either a former working partner or beau of Sapphire, possibly both - is given an added twist by Collings' effete performance. What could have been a standard clash of masculine egos is given an additional, unforeseen edge. The somewhat darker, more sinister aspects to Silver's character were also something intended by the actor: 'It was just to add another colour to it. Sort of, where do they come from? Who are they? What are they? I just wanted to sort of leave it hanging in the air, so it was not a one dimensional character. And a rivalry between Steel and Silver, the sort of dislike they had for each other.'

While it's easy to disregard Assignment Three as a 'failed experiment' like the central plot of its storyline, it rewards repeat viewings, and presents the viewer with enough ambiguities to allow it to retain its freshness. One of the most telling subtexts is that of what Silver has been doing before he joined the story as televised. As referenced earlier, we know that he's aware before Sapphire is that the occupants of the two other experiments are dead – prompting to one to wonder what involvement he had in such a development. As the final episode features Steel making a half-hearted suggestion that Eldred and Rothwyn do the same, did Silver press this further? Interestingly, the original press release to accompany the story described the character as a 'tough guy', which is largely at odds with the image Collings projects onscreen. However, there are glimpses behind what could be a façade, including his menacing description of the dead occupants to Steel: 'You don't need to worry about them. They don't matter any more.'

Interestingly Sapphire and Steel act against their perceived characteristics in the final episode. While Steel was previously presented as willing to sacrifice a human life when there was no other option, here that's taken to extremes, with him suggesting to Sapphire in a blasé fashion that they sacrifice the entire tower block population. ('They'll be saving the whole of humanity … Human beings love a good sacrifice.') There's also the scene where Steel is quite willing to murder without compunction, ready to strike a fatal blow at the base of the Changeling's neck before Sapphire stops him. Yet the conclusion sees Steel acting as the moral conscience, debating with Sapphire the right to send the couple back with the creature on board. ('But what about Rothwyn and Eldred? We can't send them back with it […] We can't!') It's a curious reversal that seems to suggest that while Sapphire understands the importance of interaction with the people they encounter, both leads put on a front for their missions.

Finally, we never learn exactly *how* communication has been cut off from the capsules to their own time. While it's tempting to presume the creature merely cut off all links to the future, it's never made clear whether or not the silent, unresponsive future has an identical problem with the remnants of animals. As the story concludes with Sapphire and Steel returning the capsule – complete with creature intact – back to the future, have they in effect condemned it to the very fate that threatened Earth in 1980?

A much undervalued piece of fantasy television.

ASSIGNMENT FOUR

EPISODE	UK TRANSMISSION	TIME	DURATION	AUDIENCE SHARE
ONE	Tue: 27 Jan 1981	19:00	23'38m	16%
TWO	Thur: 29 Jan 1981	19:00	24'19m	19%
THREE	Tue: 3 Feb 1981	19:00	24'18m	15%
FOUR	Thur: 5 Feb 1981	19:00	25'37m	20%

GUEST CAST:
Alyson Spiro (Liz), Philip Bird & Bob Hornery (Shape), Shelagh Stephenson (Ruth), Natalie Hedges (Parasol Girl) and several uncredited child extras.

TECHNICAL PERSONNEL:
Maureen Riscoe (Casting), Mike Whitcutt (Cameras), John Willment (Vision Control), Mary Southgate (Make-Up), Mary Gibson (Costumes), Ron Brown (Programme Administrator), Ann Murphy and Denise Shaw-Vance (Stage Managers), Ivor Weir (Title Sequence), Cyril Ornadel (Music), Pete Wernham (Sound), Yvonne Kelly (Vision Mixer), Al Pigden (Video Tape Editor), Ron Blanchard (Floor Manager), Jan Woolsey (Production Assistant), Jim Boyers (Lighting), Stanley Mills (Designer), David Reid (Executive Producer), P J Hammond (Writer/Series Creator), Shaun O'Riordan (Producer) and David Foster (Director). An ATV Network Production.

SYNOPSIS:
Sapphire and Steel investigate a time break in an old lost and found

shop in 1980. At an unspecified point 'several months ago', missing landlord Mr Williamson experimented with trick photography and prisms, unwittingly freeing a creature that lived in photographs. The faceless Shape entraps the landlord and one of his tenants in an old photograph, and frees children from photographs of the 1800s to join him. The Shape reveals that it can take on human guises, can move from photograph to photograph, and is telepathic.

When the time agents arrive, they find that the only remaining resident of the building is Elisabeth Owen, a night worker operating under the name Liz Duprey. In revenge for their interference, the Shape kills the landlord and his former tenant, and threatens to do the same to Sapphire and Steel as he traps them within another of his photographs. Liz helps to free them, and they once more cage him in a mirrored prism. Steel warns Liz never to have another photograph taken as the creature swears revenge on her should he ever break free. The two agents plan to bury the prism on board a sunken ship, while the children are dragged back to their own time and into the photographs from which they came.

SAPPHIRE:

As well as her usual array of powers, Sapphire is shown to be able to sense missing people in photographs (although this could just be a good sense of aesthetic), and to gain some unspecified form of information from sealed letters by waving her hand over the top of them. She also appears able to access data, or possibly just historical knowledge, by thought: in the third episode, she concentrates in order to recall the date the very first photograph was taken, which suggests that she might be accessing a wide bank of knowledge outside of herself, something that is again touched on in the final television story. This theory is given some credence by Steel in the final episode, during which they both pool their powers to create a mirror, with Steel advising, 'Think of Mercury and Silver, borrow from their minds.' This suggests that the elements operate some form of collective consciousness. This is also the only time that Mercury is mentioned in the dialogue within the series.

A clarification of Sapphire's power to take back time is also given, as she explains, 'I can only borrow time, not keep it.' She also appears to be able to sense future events. In the second episode she tells Steel, 'There's about to be a complication,' and motions towards Liz's bedroom, seconds before Liz comes out and disturbs them.

Sapphire also seems able to affect the mood and reaction of others towards her and Steel. After an initial frosty reception from Liz, Sapphire initially freezes her in position, and then places a dressing gown over her shoulders, touching her briefly. Liz's attitude immediately changes and is far more calm and accepting towards the couple.

OLD BLUE EYES IS BACK:

Although Sapphire uses her powers once in each of the first three episodes and the pulsating sound effect is heard in all instances, only in the first do her eyes glow. When she stops Liz from moving and removes the needle from Liz's record, her eyes turn violet, not the usual blue.

'HELP ME, STEEL!':

It is notable that toward the end of the story Sapphire becomes a far less imperilled character. While she struggles to take back time against the influence of the Shape, any moment of personal danger to her, such as a child threatening her with an umbrella, is immediately repelled. When she becomes trapped in a photograph in the final episode, Steel is trapped with her, and it's left to a third party to rescue them both, an act that is initiated by Sapphire's telepathic calls to Liz.

STEEL:

Steel has some form of telekinetic power, being able to open the lock and bolt of a door by gliding his hand across the exterior, as well as being able to stop a record player. We also learn something of Steel's vulnerabilities when an object he is holding is made red hot by the Shape in the second episode – Steel feels the heat and cries out in pain. Finally, there's another example of Sapphire's knowledge of Earth history eluding Steel … she has heard of genies while Steel hasn't.

THE ELEMENTS:

Steel and Sapphire debate the politics of the elements, Steel claiming it would be better for someone to wait for the break in time, rather than arrive after the event. He bemoans the Specialists that sit around doing very little (such as Lead and Silver?), while the Operators (such as he and Sapphire) have to do all the work. She asks if he would have volunteered to wait for the break in time, which could have taken 'hundreds of Earth years'. This indicates a lengthy lifespan for Steel, at least, and a different way of measuring years for them both.

PAST ASSIGNMENTS:
Steel refers to the house seen in Assignment One. 'Remember the house? It got into a picture and we destroyed the picture. We destroyed all the pictures.'

STRANGE RELATIONSHIP:
This is the story with the least chemistry of any kind between the two agents. A smile plays on Sapphire's lips and Steel gets annoyed whenever Liz describes him as Sapphire's boyfriend. The one clear reference is in the final episode when Steel explains Williamson's photography to Sapphire as 'a few cheap tricks to impress the ladies.' 'Well,' counters Sapphire with a haughty look, 'at least he bothered to impress them.'

YOU MAY REMEMBER ME FROM ...

ALYSON SPIRO:
Alyson Spiro became most famous for her later appearances in the programme that *Sapphire & Steel* was scheduled to replace during its annual summer break. By the time Spiro took on the role of Sarah Sugden in 1994, *Emmerdale Farm* had changed its name to *Emmerdale* and ran all year round. The character had actually been played by Madeleine Howard for six years previously and was eventually killed off in a fire during 2000.

Over the years Spiro has been seen in films such as *She'll Be Wearing Pink Pyjamas* (1984) and *Birth of the Beatles* (1979). On TV she appeared as Kath Borrow in *Fell Tiger* (1985), Margaret Speel in *Prime Suspect 3* (1993), Alison Gregory in *Brookside* (1989-1990) and Pascal in the *Dramarama* episode 'A Young Person's Guide to Going Backwards in the World' (1985). Spiro currently teaches drama and appeared in a July 2008 episode of *Midsomer Murders*.

PHILIP BIRD:
Sapphire & Steel was Philip Bird's first television role after an extensive career in theatre. After appearing in the programme he immediately worked with producer Shaun O'Riordan, in the capacity of director, as Jebb in the *Callan* TV movie sequel *Wet Job* (1981). Other high profile roles included Muller in *Reilly: Ace of Spies* (1983), Henri Lecoq in *Brass* (1990), Peter in five episodes of *Fresh Fields* and seven of its sequel, *French Fields* (1984-1986; 1989-1991) and Gregory Stephens in *Coronation Street* (2000-2001). Bird also appeared in the films *Virtual Sexuality* (1999), *Killing Joe* (1999), *Caught in The Act* (1997) and *Imagine Me and You* (2005). Like Spiro, Bird also appeared, in various roles, in *Emmerdale*, though is perhaps most well known for his role as the father in the first two series of children's comedy *The Wild House* (1997-1998).

BOB HORNERY:
An Australian actor, Hornery may be familiar to genre fans as the ill-fated pilot in the first episode of the 1979 *Doctor Who* story 'The Horns of Nimon' and as a water seller in the film *Mad Max Beyond Thunderdome* (1985). Many of Hornery's roles on screen have, however, been in Australia, including as Tom Kennedy in *Neighbours* during the late 1990s. His many stage roles led to a televised version of *The Importance of Being Earnest* (1992), and he could also be seen in *Thunderstone* (1999-2000), *Blue Heelers* (1995, 1997, 2002) and *Legacy of the Silver Shadow* (2002).

MISSION BRIEF:
The credits on the final episode offer 'Special Acknowledgements' to Birmingham Public Libraries, Cambridge County Record Office, Dorset County Library, Guildhall Library, The Gwynedd Archives Service, WER Hallgarth Collection, Grimsby, Hampshire County Museum, Kodak Museum, Norfolk County Library, Northumberland County Record Office, The Science Museum, Shropshire County Record Office, Victoria & Albert Museum and Wiltshire Archaeological & Natural History Society. These bodies presumably provided reference material for some of the old photographs seen in the story.

Four nursery rhymes are used in the story, 'See Saw Sacradown', 'Eeny Meeny Miney Macka', 'King of the Castle' and

'As I Was Walking Up the Stair'. 'Eeny Meeny Miney Macka' was used in the Oscar Wilde play *The Selfish Giant* (1888), but as it was passed down through oral tradition its exact origin cannot be determined. 'See Saw Sacradown' and 'King of the Castle' are also untraceable, though 'As I Was Walking Up the Stair' is the latest of the poems, being dated to 1899.

The book that Steel picks up in the first episode is D A Spencer's *Photography To-Day* (Oxford, 1936). In the final episode Sapphire can be seen browsing through the same author's *Colour Photography in Practice* (1938), and an anonymous book entitled *Optics*. In the background can also be seen a book on the Rollei brand of camera.

Sapphire & Steel specialised in a very vague, almost esoteric style of dialogue, which makes this rare moment of technobabble in the second episode all the more surprising: 'The sudden implosion of chemical molecules would cause an emission of phototonic energy which would be impossible to contain or reverse.'

P J Hammond had planned to introduce Mercury as a character if the series had gone past six stories. One consequence of this was that, for Assignment Six, Lead was omitted from the title sequence narrative and Mercury was substituted. Curiously, episode three of Assignment Four also has this revised sequence. Its use here was probably an accident: none of the production crew recall why it happened, and the sequence reverts to type for the fourth episode and for the whole of Assignment Five.

As previously mentioned, no detailed records were kept of the series' production dates. However, referring to the fourth story, Philip Bird (the younger Shape) recalled: 'Rehearsals for the programme began on 10 July 1980, recording began on 22 July and finished I think on Friday 15 August. That's certainly when I finished my bits.'

Over 60 children are reputed to have been auditioned for roles in this story, all of them selected from casting agencies and stage schools. As no records were kept, none of the child extras can be identified.

The very first object that Sapphire picks up when she and Steel explore the lost and found shop is the kaleidoscope used at the end to trap the Shape.

WHAT'S IN A NAME?

As *Sapphire & Steel*'s six television stories were untitled on screen, subsequent discussion amongst fans led to a *Friends*-style 'The one with …' describing game. The VHS releases saw them titled 'Adventure One', 'Adventure Two' and so on, with this title superimposed over the picture. For the Region 2 DVD releases, the term 'Assignment' was used.

Although many others have been devised by fans over the years, the titles now in most common use are: 'Escape Through A Crack In Time' (one); 'The Railway Station' (two); 'The Creature's Revenge!' (three); 'The Man Without A Face' (four), 'Dr McDee Must Die!' (five) and 'The Trap' (six).[4] These titles have been so often repeated over the years that (as with the claim that David Suchet performed the series' opening narration) they have sometimes become accepted as fact, even though they were simply fan creations. The alleged titles even found their way onto the Region 1 DVD releases.

There is an enduring myth that P J Hammond created unofficial 'names' for each story, but Hammond noted, 'I had nothing to do with the story titles. If I had, I think I would have tried something more interesting.' Hammond later suggested that a title he would have chosen for the second story if prompted to do so would have been 'The Girls Who Gave Them Flowers'.

GOOFS:

A great amount of *Sapphire & Steel* was recorded as long continuous takes in the studio, with multiple cameras. Occasional mistakes are therefore to be expected. Often these are just minor things, like Lumley getting an itch at the start of the second episode and trying to scratch it while in character, or Alyson Spiro getting a line wrong in the third ('I mean, they're out here playing fr– 'till all hours, and no-one comes and gets them.') However, the fourth Assignment turns out to be the most glitch-crammed story of them all.

At the start of the story, when the Parasol Girl enters the photography room to get some more children to play with, she

---

[4] Discussion of the titles has been held back until this section of the book due to the fact that the Assignment Four title could be considered a major spoiler.

places her umbrella against a cupboard, which then falls over. Without ruining the take, she bends down to pick it up as the children move to another table.

12 minutes into episode two, a shot of Lumley on the stairway sees a boom microphone shadow very obviously cross her arm. Although such things were commonplace for television of the time, this is a particularly prominent example.

Also in the second episode, McCallum and Lumley discuss a photograph that hasn't been touched for '97 years'. The following episode, they tell Liz that the photo is '87 years old'.

Lumley has a habit of placing her arms behind her back in the story, an action which, with her free-flowing dress still hanging by her sides, makes it look as if her forearms have disappeared. Although this is not a 'goof' as such, watch out for it in particular in the third episode, in the scene where she and Steel debate whether or not to burn all the photographs in the house.

In the fourth episode, 13'30m into the action, one of the child extras looks directly into the camera.

In terms of goofs within the fictional story, there's Steel looking at the Shape after he's burnt Ruth, where he sees the older Shape, not the younger one that usually appears to him. Throughout the story, it's been established that the Shape can control his form based upon who is looking at him. A possible explanation here is that with his belief that he's about to defeat the agents, he no longer bothers to maintain any excessive illusion.

Possibly the most prominent goof in the whole series occurs 24 minutes into the final episode, where an off-camera crew member starts coughing during recording. McCallum and Lumley carry on acting as if nothing's happened, despite two loud bursts of hacking. As director David Foster explained, the most likely reasons for its inclusion in the finished episode were: '[Either] by the time the sound department had pointed it out to us, we had run out of studio time, or to do complete retakes would have put too much of a load on the cast.'

THE CLIFFHANGERS:

- EPISODE ONE: As Liz tries to recall what her landlord looks like, he returns to the house to greet the children. As the camera pans upwards, it's revealed that he has no face.

- EPISODE TWO: Sapphire encounters the children as one of them raises an umbrella as if to gouge out her eye.
- EPISODE THREE: Ruth screams as she is burnt to death while trapped in a photograph.

OVERVIEW:
In *Sapphire & Steel*'s most surreal story, P J Hammond makes life easier for himself by giving us the series' only creature from outside time that can verbally communicate.

The Shape is brought to life alternately as a faceless, bowler-hatted figure (which, given how much children rely on facial recognition, is almost a cruel level of horror for a family audience), a suave, laid-backed menace as played by Philip Bird and a sadistic, taunting one that burns his victims to death as depicted by Bob Hornery.

Overall the four episodes comprise a magnificent piece of television that sees the narrative tightened in length and the earlier mannered, almost oblique, mannerisms of the titular agents restored. While Sapphire is flighty, with an elfin hairstyle and almost faerie-like dress, Steel is at his most brusque and impenetrable. After the somewhat whimsical, fantastical third Assignment, this is *Sapphire & Steel* returned to its darkest origins, and neither agent is in the mood for levity. It's possible to think of the fourth story as the most upbeat, with relatively garish shades (the final shot is of a multi coloured kaleidoscope) and a blast of loud jazz in the opening seconds adding to the sense of youthful contemporaneity. Yet *Sapphire & Steel* was always at its best when dealing with lost souls and desolate situations; and though Spiro is almost relentlessly upbeat and cheery as the archetypal 'tart with a heart', this is probably the most humourless, most remote *Sapphire & Steel* story of all. Perhaps reflecting Hammond's growing exhaustion, the episodes are shorter than usual, and McCallum and Lumley spend much of their time apart, with a real distance between them. A depiction of shattered lives and wasted opportunities around a shop that contains nothing but 'the belongings of the poor, the hopeless and the dead', the story features spiteful children trying to gouge out peoples' eyes and an innocent man and woman being burnt alive. *Sapphire & Steel* was rarely afraid to take risks, and this surreal yet ultimately downbeat story continues the tradition.

Perhaps more than any of the other stories except the last, it has a greater sense of artifice throughout, reinforcing the series' theatrical leanings. The exteriors recorded in the studio are surprisingly well realised, though unconsciously viewers cannot help but pick up on their fabricated, almost stage-like appearance. The deliberately mannered performances of McCallum and Lumley are, in the opening episode particularly, constantly framed or obscured by inanimate objects. With shadows frequently playing across their faces, this not only increases a sense of danger but also utilises the *mise en scène* to engender a subtle yet omnipresent claustrophobia.

For once, P J Hammond's influences are visible, which is no bad thing. Here the series delights in its own intertextuality, not just in its Magritte-inspired villain but in the umbrellas that attack Sapphire with the sound of crows, tearing at her flesh, her performance a nod to that of Tippi Hedren in Hitchcock's classic 1963 movie *The Birds*. What places the story beyond all this is that it extends past its roots to present arguably the most inspired concept in the whole series: a man who can live in and move between any photograph ever taken. It's a brilliantly original idea and one realised incredibly well onscreen. Visually, however, it perhaps wasn't to all tastes, as Philip Bird, the younger Shape, was later to comment: 'It did slightly bug me that in profile, Shape looks a bit bulgy, like he is wearing a mask in fact – even though face-on it is very effective. I wish I had thought about that a bit more at the time.'

A possible inspiration for the Shape comes from a British Public Information Film released in 1973 and narrated by Donald Pleasence. Titled *Lonely Water*, the 90 second commercial featured children plunging to their deaths in a river as Pleasance's haunted delivery enforced the point of view of a hooded figure with no face. His refrain of 'I'll be back' even forms part of the Shape's final haunting threats to Liz: 'You … girl … no-one hides from me. I'll find a photograph. Your photograph. I'll be back. Paper burns. Nothing lasts. Only me.' However, this is merely speculation, and similarities can be found in a variety of contemporary source texts if desired. Indeed, another series that opened with sepia photographs of children and revolved around a lost and found shop was the perennial children's favourite *Bagpuss* (1974), which saw regular repeats around the time. A source of inspiration cited by Hammond himself was the Aboriginal belief that to have one's photograph taken was to have someone steal your soul. Such concepts were partly revisited by Hammond in 2008 when he created a travelling circus that could exist in and emerge from film stock for the *Torchwood* episode 'From Out of the Rain'.

The all-encompassing nature of the Shape led to Philip Bird and Bob Hornery devising their own individual interpretations with the director and not attempting to mimic each other's take on the character. Bird observed: 'Because Shape can in theory be anyone – and therefore Bob and I were just two of an infinite series of faces that Shape could adopt – then to look for any kind of consistency of character would be against the spirit of the creation.' As with Russell Wootton in Assignment Three, casting had taken a chance in giving another guest actor his first break into television, this being stage actor Bird's debut in the medium. It's a potential risk that pays off handsomely, Bird's understated, uncaring sadism making for a pleasing contrast to Hornery's overt spite: 'It was an amazing idea – and indeed predated Woody Allen's *Zelig* by a couple of years.'

As mentioned, the most obvious influence on the realisation of the Shape were the works of Magritte, a Belgian artist (1898-1967) who produced most of his work as part of the Surrealist movement. Although Magritte had produced his last painting 13 years before the story was made, like most artists his reputation and influence had grown posthumously. He is not a household name like his peer Salvador Dali, but his works are wide-reaching enough to have affected the cultural lexicon, and his bowler-hatted men (not literally faceless, but with their features obscured) are paid homage here. Many theories abound for the derivation of Magritte's imagery, for example that the hat was an allusion to the pulp novel character Fantômas, and that his obsession with obscuring features was due to having found his mother drowned, her nightdress covering her head; yet the first of these ideas is open to question, as the bowler hat was a fashion accessory for the Belgian middle classes in the '20s and '30s. However, what is undeniable is that the bowler hat no longer had any currency in 1980s Britain. As with the use of nursery rhymes, it's the constant dislocation between the contemporary and the old that not only provides Hammond with a narrative but also gives the series the sense of the uncanny.

What's surprising with the fourth story is the rise in a sexual subtext. While Sapphire and Steel are fairly distant throughout, the entire impetus for the plot is a shop owner using trick photography to lure his female tenants into his private quarters. Even more explicit is the depiction of Liz, who first appears wearing only a sparse, semi-transparent negligee. (Before entering Liz's quarters, Steel investigates the toilet, an act that was still relatively daring for genre programming of 1981.) Liz claims her job involves her working 'all night' but does not afford her possible alternative accommodation. She wears a wig for her work and claims to have spent 'half [her] life making quick exits'. Liz's assertion that she works in a club is followed by the admission 'when I'm allowed to', leading one to the apparently inescapable conclusion that she's a prostitute. Even her relationship with her ex-landlord, Williamson, is described to Steel in terms of his sexual involvement: 'Got on with his pictures ... and he just liked to talk.' To place this into a historical context, it must also be remembered that at that time the newspapers were full of stories of 'The Yorkshire Ripper', a serial killer who had begun a five year reign murdering female victims; a reign that would continue until three months after recording on the serial ended. Indeed, this relentlessly bleak tale of a sadistic man preying on two vulnerable female characters began airing just 21 days after Peter Sutcliffe was found guilty of the Ripper's crimes. While it would be a stretch, and in somewhat ill taste, to suggest that *Sapphire & Steel* was deliberately referencing such events, it could be said that this serial was very much a product of its time.

The Shape's purpose is also quite ambiguous. We can surmise from his treatment of Liz's friend and landlord that he revels in destruction, but does he bring back the children because they feel the same? As the children are rather impotent, crumbling when touched, is he there merely to play with time? Or, given that the faceless creature surrounds himself with only minors, is he something far more sinister? Hammond denied any such metaphorical intent, stating: 'Never once did I think of the Shape as a paedophile. After all, they weren't real children, they were pieces of paper.' It's worth noting, though, that a plot element involving a child abductor was included in one of Hammond's first post-*Sapphire & Steel* fantasy scripts, the 2006 *Torchwood* episode 'Small

Worlds'. It was David Foster's belief that this element of the story was there to show that children can be 'threatening', while Philip Bird, the younger aspect of the Shape, saw it as a protective role. He envisaged that the creature had grown from childhood, 'and that perhaps his childhood represented a happier time for him. That may be why he sought the company of children, with their playground games. I saw him as a kind of guardian to the children.' The first episode has the Shape away from the shop, with the parasol girl first stating, and then begging, 'I think you'd better come home. Now. Please come home.' Where the Shape had gone and for how long was something that Philip Bird also mused over: 'I wondered [about] that, and I don't think it's idle speculation, as it is important to know as much as possible about the life of the character you are playing. I didn't imagine he was meeting anyone, but rather walking the streets, maybe revisiting childhood haunts, trying to get back to happier times. Or perhaps he just went out to get off his face.' Although not a definite forebear of the story, one of Hammond's cited influences, Ray Bradbury, had a similar regard towards children in two of the stories in the 1952 UK edition of his short story collection *The Illustrated Man*. *Zero Hour* (originally published in *Planet Stories*, 1947) has cities of children plotting to kill their parents, while *The Playground* is a nightmarish vision of their unrelenting sadism. Assignment Four is a story that has a decidedly sinister subtext, intentional or not.

One of the most disconcerting sequences in the story comes in the third episode when the Shape reveals he can hear Sapphire and Steel's telepathic communication and share in it. This comes directly after he's been able partially to block Sapphire's powers on the stairway (and after the children he lets share in his adventures have temporarily imprisoned them both). With the Shape's somewhat glib introduction, 'Excuse me, would you prefer us to communicate in this way? Only, it doesn't make much difference to me,' it suggests that such powers are trivial, almost beneath him. It's a disheartening moment for Sapphire and Steel as they realise at the same time as the viewers that this is an enemy who is not only an equal, but possibly their superior. Bird's next teasing line, 'So I'll tell you what I'll do ...' sums up the character perfectly; slightly mocking, with an underlying air of menace. Neither Bird nor Hornery forces his lines in this shared scene. Bird notes: 'The menace was in the lines and in the story; there was no need to try and add anything extra in the acting. If someone is condemning you to a grisly fate, it makes it worse if they are smiling while they do it. If the villain rants and raves, he/she reveals that he/she is human and therefore vulnerable.'

Another curious element involves the use of the series' 'triggers'. As established from the very first Assignment, *Sapphire & Steel* often ignored its own rules (as arguably all television shows should do if they get in the way of a good story), by not actually having legitimate triggers at all. Although here we have the shop owner using trick photography to open a sort of self-made Pandora's Box, it is established that the Shape was *already* in all photographs from the first photograph ever taken, and was only dragged from them and into a mirrored prison with Williamson's inadvertent meddling. The punning reference to prison/prism is only part of the theme of entrapment that runs through the piece, with everyone involved suffering constant imprisonment, even if it's just Liz being trapped through her own circumstances.

Hammond's love of the perverse in seemingly innocent fixations is perhaps best illustrated by Steel picking up a Mr Punch doll in the second episode. Though ostensibly an entertainment, it's a demonically-faced doll that beats his wife. Along these lines, the Victorian children brought back from the photographs are not innocent angels but sadists who ask, 'Can we hurt them? Oh please, let's hurt them!' As for the children's rhymes used in the story, they are, if anything, even more disturbing than those used in earlier Assignments. Hammond's skill is in choosing rhymes that are not only appropriate to the story but also evocative of the uncanny. The rhyme about meeting 'a man who wasn't there' who forever haunts the teller ('He wasn't there again today ... I wish, I wish he'd stay away') suggests a haunting. However, investigation of its source reveals that it was the work of an author, William Hughes Mearns (1875-1965), who specialised in nonsense rhyme. Another of his poems read: 'As I was sitting in my chair, I knew the bottom wasn't there. Nor legs nor back, but I just sat, ignoring little things like that.' The metre of the poem is almost identical, but the tone comical. By extracting the poem from its original context, Hammond renders it devoid of humour and lends weight to its spiritual implications.

Hammond's jet-black sense of humour is again in evidence in a scene where Liz kicks ash from under her feet ... little realising that it's the remains of her only friend. There's also an amusingly disdainful 'They never learn, do they?' from Sapphire when discussing humans mixing 'the old and the new'. In lesser hands it could almost be too ridiculous, a post-modern reference to the bizarre and extreme nature of the stories, but Lumley plays it pitch-perfect. The idea that humans should realise not to place objects of different ages together lest they bring forth an extraterrestrial creature is humorous, but Lumley gives it just the right amount of conviction.

Perhaps the most disturbing moment of all is one that is very understated: the incident where Liz crushes the small boy. The scene works within the purposes of the narrative to allow Liz finally to realise that the children aren't real, so it's easy to overlook the fact that it makes no rational sense for the characters themselves. We are shown from the beginning of episode three (the episode in which the event takes place) that the children are aware that they can be crushed like paper by humans, so the child must be aware of the danger that it's in. In order for the scene to make any logical sense, therefore, then we must assume one of two things: either the crying child is heedless of its own safety, perhaps because it is so desperate for affection that it no longer cares, or because is too young to fully understand; or the child is being forced into sacrificing itself by the bullying elder children. It's notable that not only does the eldest girl push the boy towards Liz, but she even looks on impassively after he is 'killed'. The nature of the children themselves is also in doubt. Steel refers to them as 'not alive; they're not living ... they're not ghosts, they're not images ... something in between.' It's heavily implied that they share in the Shape's power, emerging from photographs and bringing other children out to join them, as well as placing Sapphire and Steel into photographs. Again, Hammond's own take – 'They weren't real children, they were pieces of paper' – is significant in interpreting the somewhat existential nature of the characters, though somewhat at odds with Sapphire's own interpretation, 'These are ghosts before death,' in episode three.

Some interesting hints regarding Sapphire's and Steel's missions and lifespan are given in this serial. When they first meet in the shop, Steel asks 'Is this the place?', receiving Sapphire's noncommittal 'Maybe' in reply. Such uncertainty indicates that their briefs are often as vague as the series itself. Even more telling is that the story establishes Hammond's idea that the elements can live for an extremely long time, or possibly forever. In the first episode, Steel bemoans that they weren't around to stop time breaking through, complaining, 'We're too late to have prevented it happening in the first place. We should have been here earlier. Before things happen. Before things break through. Someone should be here waiting.' Sapphire directly references their extended lifespan with, 'Well who would volunteer ... simply to sit and wait, maybe for hundreds of Earth years. Would you?' While Steel's response is a musing, 'Well that depends ...,' it can be taken as confirmation that he can indeed live for hundred of years, or possibly just hundreds of years in this reality, with note given to Sapphire's specification of *Earth* years. This exchange of dialogue also raises further questions. There is a suggestion that although the powers behind Sapphire and Steel cannot be precise enough to pinpoint the exact moment of a time break, they are able to place their agents in different time periods if required. Although Hammond was not keen on the idea of the agents travelling in time itself, this would tie in with the first Assignment, which suggested that their prior mission was on board the *Mary Celeste* in the 19th Century. Also with this knowledge comes the further suggestion that Sapphire and Steel are outside of time, able to be sent in, much like the creatures they face. Finally on this theme, there is the Shape's assurance to the children in the first episode that 'No-one else on this world can send you back', which appears to confirm the agents' origin as extra terrestrial, a theme that will be returned to in the following story.

In terms of production, while the series reverts here to the darker, more shadowy imagery of the first two serials (before returning to the 'daytime' setting in the following Assignment), it's not as extreme as before. While the first two Assignments were so dark they were frequently almost in pitch blackness, the fourth has a flat, more uniform look to the lighting, and the impressive set catches a level of artifice by being, in large parts, uniformly grey. The power of David Foster's direction is illustrated strongly in the scenes where we spend several minutes looking at a still photograph of McCallum and Lumley in the final part. A lesser director would have caused the story to drag with such minimalist imagery, but Foster - who intended there to be a point of view shot from the two agents trapped in the image, but didn't have time to set it up - manages to make it work and seem natural. As the story that perhaps relies the most on video effects (though, in keeping with the ethos of the programme, always to *enhance,* rather than detract from the narrative), the said effects are strikingly effective. In particular there's the scene on the stairs of Sapphire trying to call forth the various images of the Shape, and the Shape unexpectedly appearing in Liz's mirror.

There's very little to fault in these episodes, though again Ornadel's orchestral musings are perhaps a little distracting to a modern audience, turned up far in the mix. In particular, a scene in episode one where Steel investigates a door hidden behind a curtain sees Ornadel place five percussion beats four times over to punctuate the event. However, so loud in the sound dub is the music that it goes from incidental into appearing to be the diegetic sound of knocking on the door. It also has to be said that it's perhaps not the finest of the serials from an acting point of view. Hornery and Bird are both excellent as two aspects of the same creature, while the child actors are competent if not outstanding. However, Spiro may take a little more getting used to, the higher pitch of her voice jarring slightly with the material; and Shelagh Stephenson (who has since left the profession to become a regarded playwright) comes over quite flat in her delivery as Ruth. However, watched late in the evening with the viewer completely buying into the situation, these episodes make for chilling, almost nasty, viewing. In particular, the fate of Ruth is hard to watch, for, although, as stated, Stephenson might not possess as strong a vocal talent as might be preferred, the sequence features the pained screams of an unseen woman being burnt to death.

If anything, the conclusion is even bleaker than that of the second story. While Tully was sacrificed, Liz is rendered homeless, a friendless woman with nowhere to go, haunted by the knowledge that her life may be forever in danger. Unusually, it's Steel who shows the concern for human life in this one, Sapphire's coldly brutal, 'She's dead Liz,' as she talks of Ruth, symptomatic of her lack of emotional commitment to the girl throughout. In a modern age of demographic-based television, such an uncompromising work is special indeed. In fact, while the story is Hammond's favourite, if there's an off-kilter feel to proceedings it's probably due to McCallum and Lumley playing the most aloof versions of their characters. Worlds away from their performances in the comparatively warm first story, here their reaction to the only human they meet is one of functional acceptance, nothing more.

More than perhaps any of the other stories, Assignment Four is a collection of 'moments', iconographic, almost *Alice*-like elements of whimsy certain to feature in any 'best of' lists. Because of this there are narrative issues, although these don't cause the story to be any less charming. With each 'happening' being strung together in tight progression, there's a notable slackening of the pace in the third episode, where the plot can't be allowed to progress beyond a certain point, lest it fall directly into the conclusion. As a result, the rather slight plot is 'put on hold', as it were, with over a quarter of the original material featuring Sapphire and Liz discussing the children, and Liz finding out things about the children that the television audience are already privy to. The use of the term 'original material' is apt, because the third episode's length is also bolstered by an extended reprise of the end of the previous instalment, running for just under three-and-a-half minutes. While Hammond's imaginative streak had perhaps never before stretched so far, it's clear that the volume of that imagination was beginning to be compromised. As a result, Hammond stood down for the following story to concentrate on the series finale, handing the writing reins over ...

SEASON THREE

ASSIGNMENT FIVE

EPISODE	UK TRANSMISSION	TIME	DURATION	AUDIENCE SHARE
ONE	Tue: 11 Aug 1981	19:00	25'17m	16%
TWO	Wed: 12 Aug 1981	19:00	24'03m	19%
THREE	Tue: 18 Aug 1981	19:00	23'24m	17%
FOUR	Wed: 19 Aug 1981	19:00	24'48m	21%
FIVE	Tue: 25 Aug 1981	19:00	25'12m	17%
SIX	Wed: 26 Aug 1981	19:00	25'14m	18%

GUEST CAST:
Patience Collier (Emma Mullrine), Davy Kaye (Lord Mullrine), Nan Munro (Felicity McDee), Jeffry Wickham (Felix Harborough), Jeremy Child (Howard McDee), Jennie Stoller (Annabelle Harborough), Peter Laird (Greville), Stephen MacDonald (George McDee), Christopher Bramwell (Tony Purnell), Patricia Shakesby (Anne Shaw), Debbie Farrington (Veronica Blamey), Valentine Dyall (Radio Commentator) and two uncredited extras (two servants: 'Jenkins' and an unnamed maid).

TECHNICAL PERSONNEL:
Don Houghton/Anthony Read (Writers), Maureen Riscoe (Casting), Len Penfold (Sound), Mike Whitcutt (Cameras), Yvonne Kelly (Vision Mixer), John Crane (Vision Control), John Hawkins (Video

Tape Editor), Anita Harris (Make-up), Mary Gibson (Costumes), Ron Brown (Programme Administrator), Jeremy Van Bunnens (Floor Manager), Ann Murphy and Denise Shaw-Vance (Stage Managers), Jean Stevenson (Production Assistant) Ivor Weir (Title Sequence), George Leuenberger (Special Effects), Cyril Ornadel (Music), Jim Boyers (Lighting), Su Chases (Designer), David Reid (Executive Producer), P J Hammond (Series Creator) and Shaun O'Riordan (Producer/Director). An ATV Network Production.

SYNOPSIS:
21 June 1980, and Chairman Lord Arthur Mullrine holds a party to celebrate 50 years of Mullrine International. Six friends are invited, including Mullrine's deputy chairman Felix Harborough, Felicity McDee, the widow of Mullrine's partner, and Howard McDee, her grandson. Mullrine's attempts to replicate the year 1930 act as a trigger, causing time actually to shift back 50 years and a series of murders to take place. With Sapphire and Steel additional guests to the party, they find that Time has brought back the deceased George McDee, and that Mullrine's sister Emma has been offered a second chance of happiness if she reverses the accident that originally killed him. Unfortunately, if George lives he will accidentally unleash an experimental bacteria that will destroy the human race. Determined to restore time to its correct course, Sapphire and Steel convince Emma that she must replicate the original history, in which she accidentally shot George. She does so, and time is restored, with the party once more taking place ... except this time without the two agents.

SAPPHIRE:
Sapphire's telepathic abilities are greatly expanded in this story. Whereas in Assignment Two she could tell age and life expectancy by touch, here she can also tell inner psychology and motivation merely by standing next to a subject. She calls this 'receiving information', almost as if it is relayed from another source rather than a power of her own. She is also able to sense the future, being aware of a gunshot several minutes before it happens. She traverses time for a 50-year period, though this seems to be more crossing the linkway created by time rather than being able to take time back for such a long period. She enters the house under the pseudonym

Virginia Cavendish.

OLD BLUE EYES IS BACK:
Perhaps fittingly for a story in which her powers are expanded, Sapphire gets an increased range of eye effects to go with them. In sequences of her taking time back, sensing images of the past through objects and telekinetically locking a door, we get five instances of the bright/dark blue eyes. However, the first time Sapphire uses the power in episode three it's with the alternate sound effect instead of the usual pulsating. (See Assignment One.) This sound is used again in the fifth episode when Sapphire forces the artificial door to appear. However, this time her eyes not only glow blue but turn turquoise, through to green and all the way down to mustard yellow.

'HELP ME, STEEL!':
Although she temporarily disappears at the end of the first episode, Sapphire is not only in complete control of the situation, but notably dominant over Steel, even ignoring his telepathic communications to continue a game of Bridge. Only in the fourth episode when she tries to stab herself and Steel blocks the blade with his hand is there an instance of the powerful Sapphire being under any kind of serious duress.

STEEL:
Steel is shown not to be hurt or cut by a knife in the fourth episode, and breaks it with his bare hands. He also states, 'I don't drink,' though whether or not this refers only to alcohol is uncertain – it is implied that it refers to all liquids. We also discover that Steel can produce ultrasonics by using a transistor radio, and can control a computer's functions by remote projection. Steel enters the scene under the pseudonym Miles Cavendish.

THE ELEMENTS:
Despite the voiceover at the start of every episode, neither 'Sapphire' nor 'Steel' is actually an element. In episode five, Sapphire refers to a previously-unheard-of element, 'Bronze', and shortly afterwards gives Felix Harborough the codename 'Brass'. Again, in scientific terms, neither is an element – both are alloys of

copper. Ironically two of the alternatives Felix suggests *are* actual elements: tin (atomic number 50) and platinum (atomic number 78). His other suggestion, diamond (also one of the 'elements' from the title sequence) is an allotrope of carbon, atomic number 6. From the remainder of the title sequence, then, only jet joins sapphire, steel and diamond as a 'non-element', although it consists primarily of carbon: it is created by the decomposition of wood from millions of years ago under high pressure.

When Felix asks if Sapphire and Steel are aliens, Steel replies, 'In an extraterrestrial sense, yes.' Later, Sapphire speaks about Earth, acknowledging a custom as being 'on this planet', signifying that Earth is not her own world.

STRANGE RELATIONSHIP:

In the first episode, Sapphire lies back on the bed in her and Steel's shared room and asks, 'How long would it take you to get changed?' As we later discover that Steel can get changed instantaneously, this line of dialogue (and the scene break that occurs after it) are perhaps more significant than the two playfully arguing about having to adopt the identity of a married couple.

The most overt reference to any kind of a relationship comes in episode four, when Sapphire touches Steel's face, looks him up and down, and they kiss. However, by this stage in the story they are fully immersed in the adopted characters of Miles and Virginia, so it's highly likely that they are kissing 'in character' in order to fool Time. While P J Hammond respectfully declines to comment too much on the story, as it's the work of two other writers, he does concede: 'I suppose I wouldn't have gone for the full-blown kiss.' Anthony Read, recalling the event, which took place in Don Houghton's episode, noted: 'The increased chemistry between the two leads was just the way both Don and I thought and wrote. I don't think it was a conscious decision by either of us, it simply felt right.'

YOU MAY REMEMBER ME FROM ...

DAVY KAYE:

Born David Kodeish in 1916 London, Kaye made his first professional stage appearance in 1935. Due to his small stature, he wasn't required to enlist in the armed services in the Second World War, so he spent the period touring.

While his work on screen was considerable - including two *Carry On* films (*Cowboy* in 1965 and *Convenience* in 1971) - it was for his extensive stage work that he was more widely known; The Embassy Club in London's Bond Street would see Kaye star in a new show every month from 1954 to 1968. An extremely charitable man who is reputed to have raised over a million pounds for various organisations, Kaye was awarded the MBE in 1995.

Other film and small screen roles included playing a mouse in *Alice's Adventures in Wonderland* (1972) and an Admiral in *Chitty Chitty Bang Bang* (1968) and appearances in *Juke Box Jury* (1964), *Softly, Softly* (1974) and *You Rang, M'Lord?* (1990). His final television appearance was on *Barrymore* (1991). Due to his size it was suspected that Kaye would not live long as a small child, however he passed away shortly before his eighty-second birthday in 1998.

PATIENCE COLLIER:

Born Renee Ritcher in 1910 London, she adopted Patience as a stage name and obtained her surname by marrying biologist H O J Collier.

The year she appeared in *Sapphire & Steel* was also the one in which she played her most famous role - that of Mrs Poulteney in *The French Lieutenant's Woman* (1981). An accomplished stage actress since 1932, Collier had become a member of the Royal Shakespeare Company. Her film work included diverse roles in *The Girl on the Boat* (1961), *House of Cards* (1968), *Perfect Friday* (1970) and *Countess Dracula* (1971).

Her final two roles were broadcast on television in August 1985: as Miss Stopper in 'The Copper Beeches', an episode of *The Adventures of Sherlock Holmes;* and as Maria Pavlovna in the television movie *The House On Kirov Street*. She died in London, July 1987, just over a month before her seventy-seventh birthday.

JEFFRY WICKHAM:

Wickham has had roles in numerous films, including *S*P*Y*S* (1974), *Clockwise* (1986), *The Remains of the Day* (1993) and *Ali G Indahouse* (2002). A regular face on British television for over 40 years, he has appeared in series such as *The Sweeney* (1975), *Dixon of Dock Green* (1966), *Jason King* (1971), *Yes, Prime Minister* (1987), *Peak Practice* (1998) and as Blodger in *Blott on the Landscape* (1985). One of Wickham's earliest roles was in *Doctor Who*'s 'The Reign of Terror' in 1964, with other genre work including a role in *Hammer House of Horror* (1980), a TV anthology series script edited by Anthony Read.

JEREMY CHILD:
Child has appeared in films as diverse as *Quadrophenia* (1979), *A Fish Called Wanda* (1988), *The Madness of King George* (1994), *Whatever Happened to Harold Smith*? (1999) and the movie version of *Doomwatch* (1972). His TV work includes roles in *The Sweeney* (1975), *Edge of Darkness* (1985), *A Touch of Frost* (2001), *EastEnders* (2006) and as the semi-regular Sir Alan Peasmarsh in *Judge John Deed* from 2003 onwards. His most recent screen role was as Langton in the TV Movie *Margaret Thatcher: The Long Walk To Finchley* (2008).

PATRICIA SHAKESBY:
Shakesby was noted for appearing in the very first episode of *Coronation Street* (1960), playing Ken Barlow's girlfriend Susan Cunningham. She appeared in two more episodes, and also episodes of *Z Cars* (1962) and *Dixon of Dock Green* (1965). Other roles included parts in the series *War and Peace* (1972) and *A Game of Murder* (1966). However, Shakesby's most famous role came as Polly Urquhart in 55 episodes of *Howard's Way* (1985-1989).

PETER LAIRD:
Laird's first television role was playing Chang in the 1968 *Doctor Who* story 'The Wheel in Space'. Since then he has gone on to play roles in *Z Cars* (1967/1971), *Play For Today* (1979), *The Sandbaggers* (1980), *Juliet Bravo* (1984) and *Casualty* (1998).

VALENTINE DYALL:
Born in May 1908, Valentine Dyall was most known as a voice actor, in particular as the Man in Black in BBC Radio's *Appointment With Fear* (1943-1955). Other voice credits included parts in *The Goon Show*, as Dr Noah in *Casino Royale* (1967) and as the computer Deep Thought in *The Hitchhiker's Guide to the Galaxy* (1981). He appeared as the Black Guardian in five *Doctor Who* serials (1979/1981/1983),

and played Norl in the *Blake's 7* episode 'City at the Edge of the World' (1980).

His final role was in a 1985 television version of *Love's Labour's Lost,* broadcast in January 1985, five months before his death.

MISSION BRIEF:

With another new story commissioned just two to three months after the fourth, P J Hammond was too exhausted to write it, so Anthony Read was drafted in to help supply the scripts. Read was given around a week to come up with an opening episode and storyline for the remainder, and then around three to four weeks to complete the entire story, with studios and crews already booked.

Due to the extremely tight deadlines involved, Anthony Read suggested that another writer, Don Houghton, be contracted to contribute half the episodes: 'I didn't know Don personally, but I knew his work and reputation, and the fact that we shared an agent made things simpler and quicker contractually.'

Anthony Read's estimate from his personal records is that the story was taped in August 1980, which would mean that there was a delay of around a year before broadcast.

The scenes with Annabelle playing the piano in the second episode were fabricated, with actress Jennie Stoller's hands unseen throughout, obscured by the piano itself. Stoller recalled: 'It wouldn't have been me playing the piano. [It would have just been miming].'

While the difference in tone and concept due to the change in writers was accepted by all concerned, it led to many feeling as though this story wasn't fully representative of the series. Joanna Lumley in particular wasn't keen on the time travel elements of the plot and has cited the story as her least favourite.

At just over 23 minutes, the third episode is the shortest of the entire series.

WHAT'S IN A NAME?

As with all the television stories, the fifth Assignment is unnamed on screen and in production documents. Asked what he might have called the story had it been requested, Anthony Read suggested: '"Mysterious Affair at … (whatever the house was called)" perhaps, as an homage to Dame Agatha. Or how about "Midsomer Mystic

Murders"? (Hey – now there's an interesting series idea ...)'

GOOFS:
While this is arguably the most polished production of the series, the banister that Patience Collier walks down in the opening of the final episode does manage more than its fair share of wobbling as she holds onto it. Also watch out for the climax to episode two, where Jennie Stoller accidentally grabs the limp and falling Debbie Farrington in an inappropriate place.

Finally, when 'frozen in time' during the final episode, Nan Munro can be clearly seen blinking constantly and even looking around at the other cast members as they say their lines.

THE CLIFFHANGERS:

- EPISODE ONE: Sapphire investigates the aura in the door, only to vanish.
- EPISODE TWO: Annabelle screams as she finds Veronica Blamey's dead body in a cupboard.
- EPISODE THREE: Tony is found dead with a gunshot wound to the heart. Lord Mullrine observes that if Steel doesn't solve the murders quickly, 'there won't be any of us left to care.'
- EPISODE FOUR: Howard McDee chokes to death after drinking port.
- EPISODE FIVE: Felix, infected by bacteria, dies in the library as the clock strikes midnight.

OVERVIEW:
The fifth Assignment of *Sapphire & Steel* is fun but arguably the least significant entry in the series, assembled with even more haste than usual.

Anthony Read recalled that the genesis of the serial was far from ideal, and that it was devised under fairly intense conditions: 'At the time, I was in the middle of story editing *Hammer House of Horror*, which we were making independently for ATV. David Reid, ATV's head of drama, working on the principle that if you want something done fast, then ask a busy man, asked me if I could rescue them from a crisis by writing a series of *Sapphire & Steel* in a hurry. I understood that Peter Hammond had gone sick or something. Overall, it was a very happy experience, if a slightly hairy one, when we were very, very much flying by the seats of our pants.' The theme of a race against time was one that extended from the story's origins all the way through to production. Patricia Shakesby, playing secretary Anne Shaw, observed that while it was a happy recording, studio time limits were hanging over the cast constantly: 'I think at the end we were shooting against the clock, as it were. My scenes were right towards the end, and I think somebody had a bet on that we wouldn't get them in, but we did. The read through was about a month or six weeks before. I was then sent home and came back to do it filmically on one set. Because they [recorded] it set by set, as you do when you do a big movie.' Jennie Stoller, cast as Annabelle Harborough, also recalled the short rehearsal times, but commented: 'Television's quite like that anyway.'

Read having drafted in Don Houghton to help flesh out the plot and ease the workload by writing the scripts for half of the episodes, some of Houghton's previous work is notable for its potential influences on the story. Six years earlier, Hammer Film Productions had released the eighth and final film in their Dracula series. *The Satanic Rites of Dracula* (1974) was written by Houghton (who had also contributed the seventh entry, *Dracula AD 1972*) and featured Joanna Lumley as Jessica Van Helsing alongside Peter Cushing as her father and Christopher Lee as Dracula. It's more than possible that when he learnt that he would once more be writing for Lumley, Houghton was reminded of aspects of his earlier screenplay: one of the movie's characters, Nobel Prize winner Professor Julian Keeley (played by Freddie Jones), is an 'expert in the fields of bacteriology, germ warfare and diseases of the blood' – themes that feature prominently in the *Sapphire & Steel* story. The motivation of George McDee differs from that of Keeley – whereas in the Assignment, McDee unwittingly releases viral bacteria and is later accidentally shot, in the Dracula film, Keeley is hired to wilfully create a deadly virus and is hung soon afterwards by his paymasters. Yet the plot similarities don't just lie with the inclusion of a similar scientist – the finale of the film sees a man dying from infected spores in the same way as Felix Harborough does, and the entire manor house where the film is chiefly set is consumed in the flames of an accidental fire. A final, insignificant, coincidence between the film and the serial is that both are largely centred on the 21st of the month. Though not met with wide critical acclaim and publicly slated by its contracted star for deviating so far from the original source text, *The Satanic Rites of Dracula* is of interest to anyone curious about the possible inspiration behind this Assignment of *Sapphire & Steel.*

Houghton had been one of the three men to buy out the Hammer name when the company ceased making films, and, along with Brian Lawrence and Brian Skeggs, used it to front a number of horror-themed television series. Script-editing *Hammer House of Horror* (1980), a series produced by David Reid, was Anthony Read's main job while writing his three scripts for *Sapphire & Steel.* What is probably coincidental, however, is that the plot elements that seem inspired by the Hammer film don't actually appear in any of the episodes written by Houghton, and instead feature in those written by Read. The two writers had collaborated closely in formulating the plot dynamics, so who wrote which elements of plot into which episodes ended up being somewhat random, as Read noted: 'We had great fun writing alternate episodes, rather like a game of consequences or setting each other puzzles with the cliffhanger endings ... "How are you going to get out of that, then?" I never liked writing scripts without knowing exactly where I was going, but this was an exception, and I thoroughly enjoyed the challenge of the game.'

If Houghton's 1974 horror screenplay provided some additional flavour to the serial, then the chief inspiration was a homage/parody of Agatha Christie's 1939 novel *Ten Little Niggers.* Serialised in the *Saturday Evening Post* under the title *And Then There Were None,* the book was released under that name for the first US edition in 1940. In 1965 the title was finally changed in Britain to *Ten Little Indians,* this being how Anthony Read refers to it: 'Don and I spent the day brainstorming and came up with the idea of doing a spoof Agatha Christie country house mystery, a sci-fi-cum-horror take on *Ten Little Indians.*' One curious irony is that, for a series so indebted to children's nursery rhymes, Assignment Five doesn't feature any, even though its source text was based upon one. Septimus Winner's 1868 song 'Ten Little Injuns' was reworked the following year into a popular children's poem by Frank Green, which took the title of the original edition of Christie's novel.[5]

Though direct similarities between the novel and the episodes are largely superficial (the idea had become something of a UK genre staple, having already been pulled off in *Doctor Who*'s 'The Robots of Death' and *Blake 7*'s 'Mission to Destiny' in 1977 and 1978 respectively) there are some amusing parallels, such as one of the younger guests choking to death after taking a drink at the dining table. However, one coincidental parallel concerns two of the victims musing over their fate being administered by 'two judges' that 'didn't come from this world at all'. Felicity McDee's lines of '... and then there were nine/eight' are, of course, a direct acknowledgement of the source. Also coincidentally, Joanna Lumley cited the text as a personal favourite in her 2004 autobiography *No Room For Secrets*: 'I was so taken by the plot of *Ten Little Indians* that I read it straight through, aloud, to my dormitory, by torchlight, finishing at half-past three in the morning. They blearily agreed it was brilliant.'

Despite the horror and crime aspects of the initial sources, it's notable that the Assignment adopts a more traditional science fiction tone. Both writers had worked on *Doctor Who*, Houghton on two Jon Pertwee stories ('Inferno' and 'The Mind of Evil') and Read both as a script editor and as a writer/co-writer on two Tom Baker stories ('The Invasion of Time', uncredited, and 'The Horns of Nimon'). Given that Houghton's *Doctor Who* contributions were grittier and more serious than Read's, it's perhaps something of a surprise that it's Houghton's *Sapphire & Steel* episodes that are the lighter and frothier of the two. Yet not only is the central premise of the story – that a release of lab bacteria will kill off the entire human race – as far-fetched as that in Assignment Three, but there's also the greater implication that Sapphire and Steel are aliens. Sapphire talks of 'this planet', while, when asked a direct question about their alien origins, Steel replies, 'In an extraterrestrial sense, yes.' It's also notable that Steel declares, 'I am known as Steel', to which Felix Harborough makes the uncorrected assumption that the agents' names are 'codenames'. Anthony Read regarded the alien nature of

[5] More modern editions of Christie's book change the words of the poem to 'Ten Little Soldier Boys', and all mentions of statuettes and place names throughout are altered to 'Soldier', with the book as a whole released under the initial US title.

the characters as an inherent part of the series' mythology: 'The science fiction element was there all along, I think – what else could Sapphire and Steel be but some sort of aliens?' A reading of the series seems to corroborate this: while there was no series bible, Steel refers to Helen as 'a human' in the very first story. ('We weren't given much of a briefing on the series,' claims Read. 'There was no bible, presumably because P J had written everything until then and had it all in his head.')

Also taking the adventure out of the realms of a 'real' supernatural story with a twist is the enormous increase in Sapphire's powers. Here her telepathy can tell not only the age of a person but also their innermost desires. Effectively Sapphire becomes, like the rest of the production, a work of metafiction; television showing its awareness of itself as a fictional construct. What was still a relatively unique approach in this medium suddenly degenerated into little more than a parlour trick, or a 'cheat' for the writers. The need for exposition with such a large cast is avoided by having one of the leads read out brief character resumes in the name of 'information transferral'. This increased power also gives us a portrait that can be used to glean a mental image of events that took place over 50 years earlier. It's a massive leap into full fantasy, and the associated lack of vulnerability, coupled with the lack of personal danger bestowed upon the two agents, makes the story short on tension.

While Sapphire is used very much as a plot device, Steel is far more lucid and humanistic than elsewhere. This is perhaps the major difference between the scripts of Houghton and those of Read (who otherwise manage to blend their episodes together extremely well, with few clashing elements of style): Steel is written by Read as nearer the taciturn character that Hammond devised. Houghton's third episode in particular has Steel gathering the guests round for an investigation in an almost-parody of Poirot. This is by far the most verbose that Steel will ever be in the entire series. The man comfortably holding forth in front of the entire room and dutifully holding out an ashtray for Mullrine to use is far from the terse, socially inept agent in all other stories.

In production terms, the most noted aspect of this serial is the rumoured clashes between the cast and crew and Patience Collier. Read recalled, 'Any clashes, as I remember, came from the fact that the main artistes were from different theatrical backgrounds. Patience Collier was very much "legit", and tended to see herself as a Grande Dame. Davy Kaye on the other hand was essentially a music hall comic always looking for a laugh, which tended to get up her nose.' Although he didn't get to work on this particular serial, David Foster observed: 'It is probable that stories of cast problems in the fifth story have grown somewhat over the years.' This seems to be corroborated by Jennie Stoller, who claimed: 'There wasn't [an atmosphere between the cast and Collier]. I don't remember much about [rumours of clashes] ... She was kind of quite fierce. And stood her ground. She only liked to be shot on one side of her face, I remember that.' (Such apparent eccentricities were confirmed by Patricia Shakesby, who, while not sharing screen time with Collier, had worked with the actress in theatre in order to observe: 'She always had to act behind furniture because she didn't like her ankles. One side of her face, and behind furniture, or in a long dress. You see, that's the old school; they were allowed to do this. You wouldn't be allowed to get away with that these days.')

A contradiction of such statements came in Shaun O'Riordan's remarks on the Region 1 DVD release to the effect that Jeremy Van Bunnens walked out in protest at having to work with Collier, an instance that Shakesby regarded as a possible clash of styles and ideals: 'Shaun is a very relaxed person, he's one of these directors that really knew his job, knew how to shoot something, but didn't give you a lot of input where you felt you were left sort of pretty sure of yourself. I think that some of the old school thought he wasn't strict or tough enough. I think that's possibly one of the things [that led to behind-the-scenes clashes with the main cast]. But I liked working with that kind of director; I like a director that leaves it and treats you as a professional, and I think he did.' Of Collier, Shakesby suggested: 'For somebody like Patience, she was such a grand actor in the theatre, and when you get on television it's a very great leveller. People that matter in the theatre don't necessarily matter on television. And I think sometimes the old actresses found this difficult to accommodate. I think for people like Patience – who had been brought up as a huge, huge stage star and worked with everybody, Olivier and Richardson, Gielgud, all the time – going on to do not such a starry thing, where let's face it Joanna and David were the stars, would be harder to take, because you felt like you [ought to be] treated like a diva, really. Of course, it doesn't happen on television, because half the people that work on television have never heard of you. And I think that sometimes was difficult for some of the older stars.'

Whatever the scale of any disputes on this serial, the overriding recollection of behind-the-scenes contributors is of a happy show and two stars now well into their characterisations, Shakesby noting: 'It was a very happy experience. Joanna was charming and so was David. They seemed to be getting on like a house on fire.' Stoller concurred: '[The two stars] were lovely to work with. I mean, Jo, I just think she's a wonderful human being. Generous and sweet and kind and delightful, and you know her career's gone on to prove that.'

Of the serial itself, there's the feeling throughout that the storyline couldn't sustain the full six episodes, and so various side avenues and diversions of plot are implemented to draw things out. While subplots and unforeseen developments naturally occur in drama, episode five's reinvention of Felix Harborough as Brass, a man sharing a telepathic link with the two agents, cannot feel anything but artificially grafted on. What gives the development such an ultimately hollow air is that Steel confesses he has enlisted Felix as a 'fellow agent' solely for the purpose of 'getting him out of the way ... take his mind off it.' As the character dies soon afterwards, it does nothing to advance the narrative, though must be praised simply for the fact that it's an amusing and charming diversion. In particular, scenes of Sapphire ignoring Steel as she plays Bridge and Brass responding telepathically are appealing. There's also a nice line in black humour, perhaps most accentuated during the conclusion of the Felix subplot, where Steel snaps, 'Not now, Felix,' as the dying man tries to get his attention. However, with all the murders seeming almost parodies, and the cliffhangers unfeasibly melodramatic (particularly the echo on Kaye's voice to make the end of the third episode seem more charged), it becomes dangerously close to pastiche. In this regard, Read recalled: 'The tongue-in-cheek element was absolutely deliberate. Both Don and I liked to inject a bit of humour into our work, and let's face it, it was hard to take *Sapphire & Steel* seriously.'

One thing that's striking about the story is that it contains no social realism, being little more than imaginative fancy. While

Sapphire & Steel is often saved from dating by refusing to align itself with gritty realism, the third Assignment had seen P J Hammond give the series a political voice, and the fourth was suitably desolate for the age. Yet the series was produced at a politically dark time, which it steadfastly refuses to reflect. Two months before it debuted on television, Margaret Thatcher and the Conservative government came to power, and during the screening of the third story, Ronald Reagan was elected as President of the United States. Their terms of office coincided with a renewed Cold War and an economic recession at home, situations that - while later reversed - cast a sombre backdrop over the time in which *Sapphire & Steel* was being produced and aired. Five months after Assignment Five was broadcast, unemployment in Britain would rise to over three million for the first time since, ironically, the 1930s. Yet as a pure fantasy, the series manages to sit outside the times in which it was made, only the length of haircuts or the defranchising of ATV - which saw the series' demise - having any form of contemporaneous reflection upon the programme.

A fairly unusual element of the story is that (as would also be the case with the subsequent one) there is no attempt to suggest that it is contemporary. Like the third Assignment, which was set in January 1980, the time of its recording but a year prior to its broadcast, the fifth is set in June 1980, which was already in the past at the time of recording, much less broadcast. Also of note in this story is a marked increase in sexual tone, with multiple affairs being referenced, Sapphire being called a 'bitch' and Mulrine remarking on his sister sleeping with George McDee as being 'good business'. The most notable development of this, however, is that the occasional intimation of tension between Sapphire and Steel is moved into a full blown suggestion of romance. In fictional terms, this development could possibly be due to Steel already becoming controlled by Time and becoming immersed fully in his adopted persona. As Sapphire notes of Time in this story, 'It's having to deal with us on more than one level. As Sapphire and Steel and as Miles and Virginia.' It's with this notion that the agents devise a strategy to keep within their characters in order to confuse their enemy, and so arises also the possibility that their affection and shared kiss are part of the fabricated identities. This would also explain Sapphire laughing manically while trying to stab herself. This sense that they have become lost in their adopted personas is perhaps the wittiest element of the scripts, almost a commentary on the artificial, Christie-homaging events around them. As Howard McDee observes to Steel, 'This is not a damn story. This is real!'

Another striking element of the serial is that it centres around a love triangle with a middle-aged man and two ladies in their seventies. Read recalled: 'I don't think we thought very hard about the senior citizen love triangle, either. Maybe it was because the Christie-type mystery was a rather old-fashioned form. Certainly, now that I'm a senior citizen myself, I'd appreciate seeing a bit more adult (I use the word in its old-fashioned meaning!) entertainment on the box.'

Often the actors have to contend with the varying dimensions of their roles. While all are, to an extent, clichéd, Jeffry Wickham's Felix Harborough is virtually a cardboard cut-out, an upper class 'toff' who utters such lines as, 'I'd rather know where the next Range Rover is coming from.' Wickham's performance is inspired, but he spends the first four episodes reacting against the limitations of the part. Only in the fifth, when he gets to share telepathic communication as Brass, does something genuinely original really emerge.

There are some engaging moments of ambiguity between several of the other characters to redeem this. Though we later learn that Mullrine's prim secretary Anne Shaw is having an affair with Tony Purnell, one of the opening scenes sees Lord Mullrine suggestively talking about her 'bedroom in the annex' and touching her face. It's left unclear whether Mullrine is merely a lecherous boss, or whether Shaw's place in the company is secured by her being a 'kept woman'. A nod towards the latter not being the case is Shaw's 'silly old Devil' after Mullrine leaves, but the story still persists on giving viewers the cynical representation of sex being a tool used to manipulate others. It's this level of conflict within character that elevates such roles beyond their narrow scope. Mullrine is a childlike, competitive man who delights in practical jokes, like, for example, the rigged radio, but is foul tempered when they go wrong. More notably, he's a man who uses his position to be, at the very least, tactile with his secretary, uses his own sister as a virtual prostitute and even threatens to stab George when he tries pulling out of a contract. Even the revelation of the origins of his business – a multinational company that made millions while the Great Depression crippled the world's economy – paints a picture of a selfish, self-made man. That such a character could still be likeable is a testament not only to Davy Kaye's skill at portraying both sides of his nature, but also to the clever way in which the dual nature of the character is written.

With such a large cast the serial takes the unusual move of having the titular characters often on the periphery, with them not even appearing in the story until almost halfway into the first episode. In this regard it's comparable with the third Assignment, in that the action doesn't revolve exclusively around Lumley and McCallum, and characters operate independently away from them. A trait shared by all three of the odd-numbered stories is that the climax turns out to be a 'happy ending', with events effectively reset to zero. Narratively it works, but dramatically it perhaps feels unsatisfying.

While the production values of this serial are arguably the highest of the series, O'Riordan's direction opts for a less satisfactory mock period style. Of particular note is the usage of aerial shots in a pedestrian setting, coupled with the long-outmoded inward zoom (as opposed to zooming or panning out of a shot, which is still part of modern direction currency). The succession of shots where objects are ostentatiously placed in the foreground or actors' backs face the camera sadly gives the impression of something like Victoria Wood's *Acorn Antiques* rather than an allusion to Truffaut. The staging of the piece isn't helped by the significant height differences between the cast members, many of whom are well over a foot taller than the reportedly 4′ 11″ Kaye. While Kaye's performance more than validates his inclusion, the effect his short stature has on the blocking of certain scenes is a distraction.

Perhaps, though, the way in which the fifth story most compels is in the smaller details not picked up on in a single viewing. There are charming moments of whimsy, such as the deceased Howard claiming, 'I was just watching my first day at school,' and musing over the nature of the afterlife. Best of all though is the relationship between Emma and Felicity. 'Who would have done such a thing?' asks Emma after one of the murders. 'Almost anyone in this house, Emma,' Felicity pointedly replies –

the significance of this exchange becoming apparent only when we learn later that both share the experience of Emma shooting George. With this in mind, it's diverting to wonder how long Emma was aware of what was going to happen at the conclusion of the party, Time presumably having offered her a chance at a new life before the events of the first episode.

The fifth Assignment for *Sapphire & Steel* is a superficially entertaining story that can delight greatly when watched in isolation. Only its inclusion in the wider series, particularly between two of the bleakest instalments, make it feel somewhat out of place.

ASSIGNMENT SIX

EPISODE	UK TRANSMISSION	TIME	DURATION	AUDIENCE SHARE
ONE	Thur: 19 Aug 1982	19:00	24'32m	16%
TWO	Tue: 24 Aug 1982	19:00	24'14m	16%
THREE	Thur: 26 Aug 1982	19:00	24'31m	15%
FOUR	Tue: 31 Aug 1982	19:00	24'37m	15%

GUEST CAST:
David Collings (Silver), Edward De Souza (Man), Johanna Kirby (Woman), John Boswall (Old Man) and Christopher Fairbank (Johnny Jack).

TECHNICAL PERSONNEL:
Maureen Riscoe (Casting), Bob Woodhouse (Sound), Gerry Elms (Cameras), Yvonne Kelly (Vision Mixer), Jim Reeves (Vision Control), John Hawkins (Video Tape Editor), Anita Harris (Make-up), Mary Gibson (Costumes), Ron Brown (Programme Administrator), Bill Goodall (Floor Manager, episodes 1 and 2), Ron Blanchard and Martin Essex (Floor Managers, episodes 3 and 4), Ann Murphy and Denise Shaw-Vance (Stage Managers), Glenys Collins (Production Assistant), Ivor Weir (Title Sequence), Cyril Ornadel (Music), Jim Boyers (Lighting), Stanley Mills (Designer), David Reid (Executive Producer), P J Hammond (Creator/Writer), Shaun O'Riordan (Producer) and David Foster (Director). An ATV Network Production.

SYNOPSIS:

Sapphire and Steel are assigned to investigate a time break at a roadside garage and café in late July 1981. When they arrive, they find that time has stopped at 8.54 pm and that the surrounding roadside is trapped in what appears to be a time loop. Even stranger, Silver has arrived before them and has spent around six hours investigating, although the time break occurred before any of them arrived.

The agents find the café area of the garage to be occupied by an eloping couple from 1948, and the rear of the garage haunted by the image of the owner from 1925. After investigating the place, they realise that time has jumped forward ten minutes and is now frozen at 9.14 pm. Then they are joined by another stranger, an ensemble entertainer from 1957 known as Johnny Jack.

With time jumping forward further, Silver tries to find a way out, but his journey causes him to breach an invisible barrier that surrounds the garage. As he does so, it awakens the dormant nature of the garage owner, Johnny Jack and the unnamed man – all three are agents similar to Sapphire and Steel, but answer to 'a higher authority'.

Silver speculates that they may be 'transient beings', shape-shifting creatures from the past using time travel devices to hunt agents down. Silver manages to duplicate one of their time travel devices and sends the garage owner and Johnny Jack back into the distant past. However, the unnamed man catches up with them and uses his own device on Sapphire and Steel, transporting them into another café area. With Silver's fate unknown, the man and the woman reveal that this is their final trap – they fade away, leaving Sapphire and Steel looking out of the window of the café onto an endless starscape from which they cannot escape.

SAPPHIRE:

Sapphire can project the image of a car in this story, as well as use her mental powers to make observers become infatuated with her. However, when in the third episode she brings forward time to see what will happen, it is implied that her powers are gleaned from another source: she says, 'Show me more', followed, after a brief pause, by, 'I said show me.' With her talking earlier about 'computing' how the time disturbances add up, it all seems to point towards Sapphire accessing knowledge and powers rather than having them as latent abilities. This supports the implication to that effect in the fourth story, when she and Steel created a mirror together by borrowing from the minds of other agents. Curiously, in the final episode, she says in reference to future events: 'It's my job to know.'.

OLD BLUE EYES IS BACK:

Sapphire uses her powers five times during the story, and in each case the usual pulsing sound effect can be heard. However, on two occasions - when hypnotising the unnamed man and when calling forth the images of her future - the glowing blue eye colour is not used. However, the most significant development in this area is that the unnamed woman is the only character in the series who refers to being able to see a change in Sapphire's eyes ('Your eyes ... what's happened to your eyes?') when this occurs.

The same eye effect is used for the transient beings when they emerge, though clearly without the use of special lenses as it is more muted as a result.

'HELP ME, STEEL!':

Sapphire's evolution from a feminine novice to an assured, almost wilfully aloof character comes to its logical conclusion here. Although Sapphire cries out for Steel to help her in the last episode, and she allows Silver and Steel to do much of the physical work, in many ways it's as if the she and Steel have influenced each other during their missions together. In the second episode, Sapphire is now so experienced and Steel becoming so blasé, almost naïve, that she barks, 'Think about it for once, Steel!' without hesitation. In her company, Steel has developed from the dominant, uncaring force he once was, and tried to gain greater empathy with the people they meet. Yet finding he doesn't understand human emotions, he is left trying to comprehend what's going on around him on a personal level, while Sapphire (and Silver) behave more impassively.

STEEL:

Nothing new is learnt about Steel's abilities in this story, though he is not as physically strong as the transient beings ...

THE ELEMENTS:

Silver makes a return appearance here. He exhibits the capability to open a till register and a car door without physically touching them, and once more displays the ability to reproduce objects, this time a tambourine and the protagonists' time-travel device. He also has a small wand-like device with a light at the end that enables him to rig a one-armed bandit to win every turn. The briefing the three agents receive is implied to be a spoken introduction to the missions, and they comment that this one was conveyed 'more like a kind of knowledge.'

The title sequence narration was changed by Shaun O'Riordan to omit Lead and list Mercury for this story. This was to reflect Hammond's initial idea to feature the agent Mercury in future stories, an idea that ultimately never came to fruition.

PAST ASSIGNMENTS:

Although it is never referenced on screen, could the events of this story represent Time's final revenge for Steel and Sapphire cheating it at the conclusion of Assignment Two ...?

FUTURE ASSIGNMENTS:

At the end of the fourth Assignment, Sapphire and Steel commented that they would be waiting in 75 years' time, when the sunken ship on which they buried the Shape would be due to emerge after being trapped in a 'pyramid of ice'. As both of the agents are imprisoned at the climax to the series, then what will happen to the Shape when he is due to break free in 2055?

STRANGE RELATIONSHIP:

With Silver returning for another mission, there are few instances of visible attraction between Sapphire and Steel, as the technician seems to constantly come between them. This is significant in that Steel's abrupt nature is made even more volatile, and he is noticeably resentful of Silver and Sapphire. Due to this, Silver and Steel constantly play off one another from the very first minute they meet, Silver claiming he hadn't interviewed the couple because 'I thought I'd leave that to you – I'm not very good with intimidation.' He edges Steel away from the one-armed bandit he has been unsuccessfully playing, and with a little trickery manages to win the jackpot several times, amusing Sapphire.

Later, after Sapphire links with Silver's mind, he kisses her palm, then places it on his cheek and onto his heart. Talking about the two strangers in the café, Steel remarks, 'Let's find out some more about those two as a loving couple'. This is met by vague looks from Sapphire and Silver, causing Steel to elaborate: 'Well, they are only human, aren't they?'

In the second episode, Sapphire toys with the male stranger by using her powers to make him, apparently, infatuated with her. Silver breaks her gaze by cutting in front of her with an irritable 'Excuse me', either jealous or angered at her unethical misuse of her powers, or both. It is notable however that Sapphire does not trust Silver in a hostile situation and asks Steel if they should do so - and while in danger during the final episode, she finally allows her eyes to play fondly over Steel's face.

YOU MAY REMEMBER ME FROM ...

EDWARD DE SOUZA:

RADA graduate Edward De Souza was born in 1932 and had early TV roles in, amongst other productions, *The Avengers* (1963/1969), the *Doctor Who* episode 'Mission to the Unknown' (1965), *Rocket To The Moon* (1967) and *Department S* (1970). Film roles came in *The Phantom of the Opera* (1962), *The Thirty-Nine Steps* (1978), *The Spy Who Loved Me* (1977) and *Jane Eyre* (1996). As well as featuring in many TV dramas from the 1970s to the 1990s, including *Boon* and *The Sweeney*, De Souza could also be seen from 1989 to 1990 as the regular character Sam Greenland in the sitcom *After Henry*. More recent appearances have come in *New Tricks* (2006) and *Rome* (2007).

During 2009, de Souza became the most widely-recognised guest star to have appeared in *Sapphire & Steel* as he took on a high-profile role in ITV's flagship soap opera *Coronation Street*. His character Colin Grimshaw debuted in December 2008 and became involved in major storylines before being killed off in May 2009. De Souza's celebrity from this role also led to him making an appearance as himself on *Harry Hill's TV Burp*.

One connection with the previous Assignment is that when the BBC decided to resurrect the Man In Black for radio in 1988, Valentine Dyall, the original title character had passed away and De

Souza was given the part instead. Another coincidence is that shortly before he appeared in *Sapphire & Steel*, de Souza played a character called Steele in the 1979 television movie *One Fine Day*.

CHRISTOPHER FAIRBANK:
Two years after recording his *Sapphire & Steel* appearance, Christopher Fairbank began playing his most noted role of Moxey in the popular comedy drama *Auf Wiedersehen, Pet* (1983-1986). Although that show was discontinued after two series for Central (ironically, the television station that was a factor in *Sapphire & Steel*'s demise), public affection for it was so great that the BBC later resurrected it, with two new series broadcast in 2002 and 2004.

Other television work included roles in *Agatha Christie's 'Murder with Mirrors'* (1983), *Spender* (1991), *Prime Suspect 3* (1993), *Crocodile Shoes* (1994-1996), *Invasion: Earth* (1998) and *The Scarlet Pimpernel* (1999). Film work included parts in *Batman* (1989), *Hamlet* (1990), *Alien*^{3} (1992) and *The Fifth Element* (1997). Fairbanks' most recent TV appearances have come in shows including *Merlin* (2009), *Ashes To Ashes* (2008), *Tess Of The D'Ubervilles* (2008) and *Law & Order* (2009). He has also completed a role in the motion picture *Goal! 3* (2009).

JOHN BOSWALL:
Now in his late eighties, John Boswall has enjoyed a career that includes roles in such high profile films as the *Pirates of the Caribbean* sequels *Dead Man's Chest* (2006) and *At World's End* (2007). He also played Goldstein in *Nineteen Eighty-Four* (1984), Barrow in *3 Men and a Little Lady* (1990) and Father Léo in the Michael Caine-Norman Jewison film *The Statement* (2003).

On television he has appeared in series including *The Hound of the Baskervilles* (1982), *Eastenders* (1990), *Wish Me Luck* (1989) and *The Uninvited* (1999) and in the TV movie *Hogfather* (2006).

MISSION BRIEF:
David Collings has recounted that there was a completely ad-libbed scene between himself and Joanna Lumley during the making of this story, however he cannot recall which it was. The most likely candidate occurs 14 minutes into the third episode, where Silver begins with, 'When we've done this, I'm going to walk out there to

where those traffic sounds are.' Lumley's initial reactions seem mildly off track here. However, David Foster's recollection of such events was: 'We had no unscripted scenes, though occasionally it was necessary to ad-lib around a situation to make a bit of business work better. I cannot remember any particular scene where this happened.' Collings confirmed that this happened during a scene with the car by recalling: 'We were under-running a bit, so David [Foster] said "Can you improvise a scene with Jo? We won't tell her." We had to hide behind this car at one point – "Improvise a little scene, see what happens." She went along with it ... I sort of devised this little flirtation scene behind the car. They said it'll just be a couple of minutes long – two or three minutes long – as the show was under-running.'

Although this story set out to be contemporaneous with the date that it was due to be broadcast, due to the delay in transmission, it ended up being a year behind when it was finally aired.

As with all of the serials, no records of production dates have been kept. However, the design plans for this Assignment list 'VTR Dates' of 20-23 November 1980. While this would probably refer to only a section of the recording schedule, it gives some idea as to when the serial was being made.

Product placement features prominently in this story, but all to give the correct 'feel' to the setting rather than for advertising purposes. Brands seen include 7UP (est 1929), Access (est 1972), American Express (est 1850), Barclaycard Visa (est 1977), Bluecol antifreeze (est 1937), Carte Blanche (est 1964), Castrol GTX (est 1909), Champion spark plugs (est 1908), Coca-Cola (est 1885), Dunlop (est 1888), HP Sauce (est 1896), India Tyres (est 1898), Kit Kats (est 1935), Lucas (est 1875), Luncheon Vouchers (est 1954), Marlboro (est 1902) and Tizer (est 1924). While there is absolutely no suggestion that the products in question were inserted in return for financial recompense, such an approach might nevertheless cause a programme to be censured by television regulator Ofcom if attempted today. On the other hand, while the products are glimpsed constantly throughout the story, even in close up, the fact that no character references them means that this could possibly fall under the 'Passive Presence' exemption in Ofcom's 2005 guidelines.

It's implied that Silver and Steel teleport in the final episode in order to reach Sapphire so quickly, though this is not confirmed as the scene does not necessarily take place in 'real time'. In all, throughout the series (disregarding the 'fade outs' at the end of their second mission, and another implied instance in the fourth story with Steel), the number of actual onscreen teleportations comes to 18. Sapphire uses this power nine times, Steel six and Silver three. Perhaps expectedly, the Assignment with the highest number of teleportations is the SF-heavy third. Even disregarding an implied instance in the second episode where Steel gets to the top of some stairs with considerable speed, there are ten separate instances of it during the story.

The car featured is a Triumph Mayflower, registration DXL 481. In the fiction of the story, it has 20,108 miles on the clock. Of the scene of the vanishing of the couple from the car, David Foster recalled: '[It initially] rose slightly on its suspension [when the two actors got out], so as the couple vanished, the car appeared to move to a different height against the background. We had to carefully load it with stage weights to lower it until the transition was imperceptible.'

GOOFS:

There's a noticeable blemish on the left of David Collings' bottom lip that make-up hasn't been able to fully cover.

During the first episode, the tomato ketchup holder on the café table changes position several times despite never being used.

After going outside in the rain at the end of episode two, Steel comes back in the following episode and is still dry. Maybe the elements can't get wet?

At 12′ 47″ into the second episode, during David McCallum's line 'We were on some sort of a countdown,' an off-camera disturbance can be heard.

In the third episode, Johanna Kirby is replaced by a 'shadow' before she fades back into shot. Not only is the 'shadow' badly aligned, it's in a completely different pose from the one the actress is adopting.

In the same episode, the noise from Johnny Jack's tambourine is unsynchronised with Silver's probing. (In fact, it starts before he even touches it.)

A double goof occurs 6′ 45″ into the third episode, perhaps

indicating the rushed nature of recording. First, Johanna Kirby is notably late with her 'What?' cue, causing Joanna Lumley to speak her 'That you've been brought here from the past and trapped here?' line over the top of it. This coincides with a boom mic shadow appearing on Kirby's left arm, then another playing over Christopher Fairbank's body. Although such shadows were fairly commonplace in television of the time, this just eclipses the example in Assignment Four as their most prominent appearance in *Sapphire & Steel*.

Lastly, director David Foster noted a sizeable goof in the story relating to the petrol prices: 'As we were recording, petrol prices were going up almost weekly. To try and keep the garage itself "present day" we guessed at the price petrol might have reached by the time the episode was transmitted. Because of the delay in transmitting that story, by the time it went out, the price in our garage was ridiculously cheap. Another warning against playing around with time!'

THE CLIFFHANGERS:

- EPISODE ONE: After Sapphire receives a premonition of fear and violence, a time shift sends the agents forward ten minutes in time. Steel questions what they are moving forward to. 'To whatever is going to happen ... here ...' Sapphire replies.
- EPISODE TWO: The shadow shape of a man approaches Sapphire ominously.
- EPISODE THREE: As the transient beings reveal their true forms, Sapphire has a revelation for Steel: 'I think they answer to a higher authority.'

OVERVIEW:

Assignment Six was the final televised story of *Sapphire & Steel*. It's perhaps fitting for such an enigmatic series that there is as much mystery surrounding its demise as there is around the fate of Sapphire and Steel themselves.

Various parties have offered up explanations. P J Hammond claims it was simply a natural progression: 'At the time, I felt that the series had run its course and I wanted it to finish as it had begun, with even more mystery. This decision was certainly compounded by the knowledge that ATV would be winding down and by the fact that the leading artists had other work commitments. There was of course speculation between the producer, the artists and myself about a possible continuation sometime in the future, but nothing was really planned.'

David Foster, director of the serial, believed that ATV's closure had a greater bearing on the decision: 'At the time, Margaret Matheson took over as Head of Drama [at Central]. She had made her name as the producer of a very thought provoking play about boys coping with being sent to Borstal [*Scum*, 1977]. She decided that [Central's] drama should show a stronger account of real life, and that fantasies such as *Sapphire & Steel* were out of place. It was only when she had re-vamped the drama "look" for Central that she put out the last episode.'

David Collings believed that the series had the potential to run for a third series, and was at one point scheduled to do so with him in every story: 'Another series was planned, with me being in all of them. But that fell by the wayside. They asked if I would do another series for them and I said, "Yes, fine," but then suddenly it all collapsed. And I think maybe David [McCallum] didn't want to do anymore, or he was making too many demands or something. So I'm afraid the third series never happened. I think it was just too much of a problem, and so they pulled it, which was a shame. [The idea of carrying on] wasn't a problem from my point of view, as it would have been very nice to do another series. I got on very well with Jo; well, with David as well; I got on with everybody.'

Although *Sapphire & Steel* wasn't particularly plagued by rumours of behind-the-scenes friction, such topics are the mainstay of tabloid journalism. However, they are not always to be believed. For instance, David McCallum famously acquired a reputation of being on bad terms with his *Man From U.N.C.L.E.* co-star Robert Vaughan, but Vaughan noted in his 2009 autobiography *A Fortunate Life*: 'Actually, we got along famously. [...] We're good friends to this day.'

Whatever the full details behind the termination of the series, *Sapphire & Steel*'s sixth and final Assignment had the undignified fate of airing a full year after the fifth. The series had been off air before – for the whole of 1980, and a smaller five month gap between the fourth and fifth stories – but this artificial curtailing of the run damaged the impetus of the show. With just four episodes - or two weeks' worth - left unscreened, there wasn't enough new material to effectively advertise, and the audience share was down as a result.

Hammond's return to the series as writer brought it back to the downbeat and oblique style with which it was associated, but the rushed nature of the scripts and uncertainty surrounding the ending - including behind-the-scenes discussions about the possibility of Silver being trapped with the titular agents at the climax - caused many delays. The scripts were reputedly rewritten quite heavily, with David McCallum taking a strong interest in this process. The tradition of McCallum and Shaun O'Riordan taking hands-on involvement in the final scripting process, often with Hammond and Foster advising, was one that was accepted by Joanna Lumley, who chose not to get involved in the extensive conferences that took place. Christopher Fairbank, who played Johnny Jack, recalled: 'Joanna Lumley apologised to all of us about the quality of the scripts, and there were a lot of re-writes.' However, while the relationship between Lumley and O'Riordan can be characterised as a friendship tempered with a productive friction, David Collings was less enamoured of the delays: 'David was the main one with all the rewriting. I mean, he wanted to change every single line. You'd do it, and then it would be even more confusing. Most of rehearsals would be spent in just rewriting the dialogue, which must have infuriated the writer. I liked [P J Hammond], we got on very well, and I used to get a little worried that we were really destroying his scripts a bit, but he was very sanguine about it. He came and he would help with the rewrites as well, and they would all work in closure.' However, Collings recalled that such delays didn't affect the on-set atmosphere, as any production difficulties were tempered with 'just a lot of laughs, a lot of joking, mucking about.'

The series' growing reliance on special effects similarly caused many delays. The time required to set up effects shots cut into the rest of the recording. Edward de Souza had to perform two takes on the walking-through-the-'glass-door' shot, and Fairbank noted: 'It seemed to take a long time to be blown backwards by a wind-machine onto a blue screen background.'

With all this in mind, it could be said that *Sapphire & Steel* stopped at just the right time before it passed its peak. While Assignment Six can be seen as a strikingly brilliant piece of cult television and one of the finest of the series, there are odd touches that point towards the series possibly being about to drift away from its original high benchmark. For a start, there's Silver's musical theme. Like the flute refrain that tried to convince viewers of *Star Trek* that every barbed comment between Spock and McCoy was the work of the Bard himself, here a tinkling seven-note stanza is used to punctuate every quirk of Silver's. Before the four episodes have finished the whimsical tune has appeared no fewer than 14 times. Again, it can be seen that styles of incidental music in the late '70s/early '80s were significantly different from those of today, particularly in volume. While Ornadel's work was exemplary for the first two stories, it becomes increasingly bombastic and ubiquitous as the series progresses. None of this was particularly noticeable at the time it was broadcast, but the growing prominence in music reaches its logical conclusion with Assignment Six's third-episode cliffhanger played out on a bass drum. These more blatant musical motifs extend to a banjo and a tambourine being used to underscore every appearance by Johnny Jack; a deeply unfortunate decline from earlier stories.

There are also odd touches of a slightly cartoonish element creeping into the series - be it Silver's silver waistcoat, the increasing use of video effects, Edward de Souza crashing through a glass door or time-travelling chess sets, which are almost a surrealistic step too far. None of which is bad in and of itself - the final story is a very fitting end - but it's an indication that had the series continued for seven, eight or even nine stories then it might have ventured into unintentional self parody. Perhaps most significant of all is that this is the point when the series started to look in on itself, leaving itself nowhere to go. Whereas previous Assignments had focussed on the dead of war or the horror of vivisection, this was a self-contained story that relied only on the series' own mythology. With the final revelation that the enemies of Sapphire and Steel answer 'to a higher authority', there was effectively nothing left for the series to do short of revealing all its secrets, which of course were the main reason why it was so intriguing, fascinating and original in the first place.

There are many wonderful elements in this final outing.

Stanley Mills' set for the story is again outstanding for the budget and period. The shaky, pseudo-*Touch of Evil* tracking shot that opens the piece reveals a garage forecourt, a café area, an extensive hallway, a service area and a rear garage. Later sequences show surrounding fencing and trees and two detailed petrol pumps with a large awning. Only the lighting - far brighter than that for P J Hammond's previous stories - and the fact that this had to be Britain's cleanest garage, with not so much as an oil spill on the floor, detract from what is another exceptional piece of production. Of course the unexpected cleanliness could have been deliberate, providing a hint that all was not as it seemed.

The sense of inescapable fate is played out from the first episode, a feeling of gripping destiny not dissimilar to the dread of the future experienced in *The Twilight Zone* episode 'Nick of Time'. Coincidentally the latter was also centred around a 1940s/50s-style American diner, though there the setting was contemporaneous. This is not to suggest that *Sapphire & Steel* was paying homage to that earlier genre series, incidentally, as the two are quite dissimilar in every other respect. Similarly, despite nostalgia clippings in TV listings magazines pigeonholing *Sapphire & Steel* as 'ITV's answer to *Doctor Who*', the two were really nothing alike. Russell Wootton from the cast of the third Assignment even goes so far as to comment, 'Of course, it *wasn't* science fiction. The term was not to be uttered. It was "other-dimensional".' Indeed, *Sapphire & Steel* is almost unique in television in being so original it's almost devoid of tangible influences.

One of the delightful aspects of the story is that it doesn't really make any sense - despite it being the only story P J Hammond wrote with a pre-planned ending. That ending sees Sapphire and Steel caught in a final trap from which they can apparently never escape. It's a suitably downbeat climax for a series that specialised in twisted fate, but does rather beg the question as to why the initial set up in the café was required. Apart from the fact that it would have made for a far shorter story, there's no real logical reason for it. After all, the two agents are not trapped by force, and the interval spent waiting for all the transient beings to arrive is not necessary when all of them can travel in time. Many such moments litter the screenplay, with Hammond placing the importance of effect over that of narrative logic. Questions such as how and why the telephone rings with a disembodied voice (oddly reminiscent of the Beatles' 'Revolution 9') are never answered, being raised only to unnerve.

Another conundrum is that the agents aren't able to sense that the café residents are transient beings before they reveal themselves. In fairness, this is acknowledged early on between Steel and Sapphire ('Do we believe them?' 'We can always do tests.') indicating that the biological test Sapphire performed on Tully in the second story is something that is possible, just something not performed in this instance. The real problem then lies with the non-Hammond written Assignment Five, which showed Sapphire being able to tell intricate details about people just by standing near to them. It's possible that the transient beings are cloaked from the gaze of the other agents, of course, with their real identities and memories being awoken only if someone tries to breach the barrier. Yet such considerations do not detract from *Sapphire & Steel*; rather they enhance its appeal. It is a series that frequently eschewed plot in favour of atmosphere and tension. In fact, this element creates a rather fascinating subplot in that the café visitors could be conditioned to genuinely believe in their own fictitious back-stories until the appropriate time.

One real pleasure the story presents is in trying to decipher the real identities and motivations of the adversaries. *Sapphire & Steel* is possibly the only programme so wilfully enigmatic that four guest characters can be introduced without any of them revealing their names. Perhaps the most compelling character is the non-transient woman played by Johanna Kirby. As the story ends with her telling Steel, 'Actually, you can [believe me], for once,' then we must assume that she was part of the plot the entire time, and that her reactions in the previous episodes – including telling Steel that she wanted to betray her male friend – were part of the subterfuge. Yet none of this ties up with the revelation that she has what appears to be two electronic circuits attached to her upper chest, which, when removed, cause her to repeat herself and behave like a disabled automaton. The fact that we can also hear mechanical whirring during this moment leads to the unusual suggestion that she may be, in fact, a robot. However, as the chief transient is aware that one of the circuits has been removed, this could also indicate that she has merely been electronically tagged or controlled in some way to ensure her loyalty. Also of note is that Sapphire appears to have some 'female intuition' about Kirby's character, and the two instantly dislike one another. Even the nature of the trap itself is left suitably hazy, with Kirby's character revealing in the last episode that the roadside garage is made up of three buildings in one, with the café area (which we finally see by itself in the closing shots) being an isolated building in 1948. At this stage there is no reason to disbelieve the explanation, and the three buildings being from three different time periods would account for the time shifts - presumably the garage elements must have come from 1925, with some unspecified area being the 1957 period. Such a setting also leads to fun speculation as to why the production has suddenly placed a whirring sound on the telepathic communication of the three agents ... Perhaps the barrier that surrounds the place produces this side effect?

Then there is the suggestion that the adversaries might be 'transient beings'. There is no confirmation of this, only Silver's speculation, so their origins and real purpose remain in doubt. One possibility is that they are the Transuranics - which would explain the need to have the café suspended in time, so that they can be used where life isn't present, as noted in every title sequence narration - yet presumably Sapphire, Silver and Steel would recognise the elements they once described as 'unstable'. Hammond's succession of inspired enemies for the agents has seen them evolve from sentient patches of light and darkness, to animal kind, through to a humanoid creature, and ultimately into antagonists even more advanced than Sapphire and Steel themselves. What we do learn from the screenplay is that the transient beings *do* exist, whether represented in the story or not. They are shape-changers trapped with no means of moving in time, described by Steel as 'locked in the past, where they belong'. This seems to indicate that they have somehow been imprisoned by whatever forces the elementals report to. Sapphire's observation that they report 'to a higher authority', and Silver's guess that they may have been 'recruited', indicate a force at work that has overridden their commanding force and used the transients to conspire in their destruction. One final speculation relates to the fact that when the transients reveal their means of travelling in time - a small boxed device that fits in the palm of the hand - the era they threaten to send Silver to is the Triassic period. Are we then to assume that this is the era from which they themselves have come; that the time device is set to an instant return to their own period? If so, are these 'shape changers' locked in the past then the dinosaurs of our own history? It's a stretch, but one along the series' own lines of logic. However, such discussions disregard the fact that even P J Hammond himself didn't quite understand his own scripts for the final story, and that character developments came as a surprise to him as he wrote them. As with the best of the series, ambience, vague explanations and enigmatic dialogue more than fill in for plot logic or strained exposition.

On the subject of mythology, there are some interesting additions to the previously established principles of the series. Earlier stories have been ambiguous as to whether the agents travel in time or whether they are immortal, but here we learn in the first episode that Sapphire regards (or at least describes) July 1981 as 'the present'. Adding to this, it is revealed that both Sapphire and Steel were offered positions with a 'higher authority' but turned them down. Also significant is confirmation that their missions are usually verbally briefed, with Silver's naggingly vague, 'It wasn't an actual briefing, not the usual. It was more a kind of knowledge.' On hearing this, Sapphire and Steel compare notes on their own briefings for the unusual mission, revealing that while they may be assigned as a partnership, they aren't necessarily assigned together ... or at least, not in this instance.

The casting of the story is up to the usual standards for the series, and a particular highlight is Christopher Fairbanks' wonderfully measured turn as Johnny Jack. The concept behind this character lies with the Mummers' play, a form of traditional English performance that is believed to date back to medieval times. Usually a tale of good versus evil, such a play would have Johnny Jack appear at the end to collect donations from the audience, with the explanation that it was for 'all the children' on his back. Bringing such a character into a science fantasy story, in which he is said to have originated from '250 different places', is another bizarre stroke of inspiration from Hammond, and the casting aids it immeasurably. One of the most famous guest stars to have appeared in the series for the work he did in later years, Christopher Fairbank recalled: 'At that time in my career, everything was a learning experience.' The relatively comfortable lead times for the making of the first series were now long gone; Fairbank observed that any cast input into their characters was restricted to 'only as much as limited rehearsal would allow.'

The subtle undercurrents of Johnny Jack are well brought to life, and it's easy to forget that Fairbank appears for less than half the story's runtime. In particular, the interplay between Jack and Sapphire in the third episode – where Sapphire has become aware of his true nature but tries to hide it, while he is suspicious but also keeps up the pretence – is wonderful. The character is also observed to be intriguingly sordid in the programme, Johanna Kirby's unnamed woman at one point asking her lover: 'Hey, are you going to leave me in there with that freak?' 'Why, what's he done to you?' 'Well nuthin' ... it's what he might do.' Although speaking with an accent similar to his own made this part easier 'but less interesting' than others for Fairbank as an actor, the opportunity to play such a threatening character conversely made it more engaging for him.

Another addition to the cast was David Collings, returning as Silver after his initial appearance in Assignment Three. While it was originally intended for Silver to become trapped along with Sapphire and Steel, this was amended prior to recording, so his apparent freedom at the end helps to inform his actions earlier in the story, leading to possible answers to the question: what happens to Silver after the others have been disposed of? Presumably the head transient could travel back to rescue Sapphire and Steel, but he initially chooses to spends time with them in the 'nowhere' café. What would Silver be doing while he waited for the head transient to return? Is the implication that he would have no means of escape anyway, so could be left unguarded, or is it something more sinister? Collings was aware that the change in the script made it appear that Silver may have collaborated with the enemy: 'They were suddenly whirled away into outer space or something, and then I wasn't actually in it, it went without me. They worried if I knew it was going to happen, perhaps connived in it happening.' Silver remaining out of the trap also took away a possible means of escape for Sapphire and Steel: 'I think partly they didn't know how to actually end the story, and that left it open-ended for them getting them back and doing another series. And that's when it all went wrong and there was a sort of general falling out. Not with me, I wasn't involved in any of that, but that was why they ended it that way I think.'

Whatever the reason behind the climax, the onscreen sparks between Silver and Steel add much to their complex relationship, Silver appearing to be less enigmatic than in their first encounter. Despite a lack of suggestion that Silver is in any way cognisant of the trap itself, what is clear is that neither Sapphire nor Steel fully trusts him. As early as in the second episode, Sapphire wants to confer about Silver's motivation when he's not present, and in the final instalment Steel gives a nervous 'Silver …' as he holds the time device in his direction. What is confirmed is that, whether or not he has actively solicited it, Silver is offered a chance at registering with the 'higher authority': the older man/transient says to him, 'I can help you, Silver. I can't help [Steel], but I can help you. It's his time, you see, and Sapphire's, but not necessarily yours.'

Unusually, it's Steel who acts as the moral compass in the story, Sapphire having a tense, distrustful relationship with the woman, and Silver disregarding her altogether. It's left to Steel to assert, 'They're using her. We have to help her, it's our duty.' As touched upon in Assignment Three, there is perhaps an indication that both agents put on 'fronts' for their missions; Sapphire the aloof agent who uses human interaction merely as a means to an end, Steel the one who internally feels the need for it, but doesn't quite understand how to achieve it. With this Assignment, his regression into something of a man-child is complete. Always a step behind his two compatriots, he is at turns bewildered, naïve and out of his depth, a far cry from the man who tolerated Sapphire as his novice when the series began. His incomprehension of complex emotions is charming, and what could be perceived as an openly hurt reaction to the flirtatious relationship between Silver and Sapphire is almost painful to watch.

The viewer feels perhaps a slight sense of sadness when watching Sapphire show emotion towards Steel in the opening moments of the final episode. As they have shared most of their screen-time in the story with the flamboyant Silver and four strong guest stars, it affords one of the few chances to see them together one last time. After everything the two have been through over the previous three years and 33 episodes, it's an all-to-brief opportunity to say goodbye. In today's climate, such casting would appear contrived: although neither star would tap into the exacting youth culture of modern television (McCallum was well into his forties when the serial was made), they were both still highly photogenic 'sex symbols' of the screen. That it avoids such a pitfall, and that McCallum and Lumley share their vehicle naturally with the guest cast, is commendable. The agents' final place of entrapment, while intended to be a prison for eternity, perhaps has a more horrific implication: while Steel has been shown not to drink or sleep during the series, it was established that another element, Lead, needed sustenance. Without food or water, how long would Sapphire and Steel survive?

Lumley has expressed discomfort with the idea of the agents being trapped forever, and often wished that they could have revisited the plotline. Ideas for possible continuations were vaguely in place, with two 'get outs' inserted within the plot and the production. The first involved the character Mercury, referenced in the title sequence in place of Lead after actor Val Pringle had returned to America. Though this character was considered only in general terms, and none of the production team can quite recall who first mooted the idea of recreating the credits with his/her name in them, the possibility was signposted for the introduction of an external element to free Sapphire and Steel. The second, even closer to home, involved Silver. As mentioned, David Collings' character was originally scripted to be trapped in the café with Steel and Sapphire, leaving open the possibility that he could perhaps use cutlery and other objects to create one of his time/space-bending devices. However, McCallum objected to this scenario on the grounds that it would be more dramatically satisfying if just the titular stars of the series were trapped in the final sequence. Despite tensions in getting the scripts revised, and P J Hammond disagreeing with the decision to write out Silver, the changes were made and any obvious solution to their plight was removed. Further ideas later discussed in vague terms for a continuation of the series involved the return of the Shape, a war between the elements and the transient beings, and a straight reprise from the closing café sequence. Despite this, and a new series being discussed as recently as 2006, such ideas have so far not been taken up, and the TV series remains discontinued to this day.

In all, Assignment Six was another excellent story with a

fittingly downbeat ending ... and while it fixed the series in audience's minds as one that was brief, it did at least stand as a fitting testament to a production team that were interested in quality over finance, and one that knew to quit while ahead.

AFTERWORD

Twenty-five years after *Sapphire & Steel* last aired, direct references to the programme still occasionally appear in the media. Perhaps most notable of all came seven years after the series ended, when Joanna Lumley was employed as a guest host on the BBC One early evening chat show *Wogan*. In an edition aired on 18 September 1989, David McCallum appeared as a guest, coming out from the wings to the strains of the *Sapphire & Steel* theme tune. Although McCallum was there to promote his new drama *Mother Love*, his eight minute slot was filled with a surprising amount of references to the programme, including a clip and McCallum's joking suggestion that he and Lumley film '*Sapphire & Steel* on ice.'

During 1992 and 1993 the series was finally released onto home video, with the first two stories later re-released, and in the mid 90s it was repeated on the Bravo channel. In October 2001 the series reached number 7 on Channel 4's *Top Ten Sci-Fi* special, with P J Hammond, Shaun O'Riordan and David McCallum amongst the 'talking heads' featured. Less than a year later, in June 2002, a computer adventure game named *Darkfall* was released, featuring a faithful recreation of the train station from the second story.

As recently as February 2009, writer Toby Whithouse placed an explicit reference to *Sapphire & Steel* in his BBC3 comedy-drama show *Being Human*. The fifth episode saw trainee ghost Annie (Lenora Crichlow) attempt a haunting with the lines 'I am darkness. I'm death. Vengeance and fury. Fire and blood. Diamonds and bones. Sapphire and ... steel.' In May of the same year, Joanna Lumley talked about the series on the *Friday Night With Jonathan Ross* chat show. This saw her refer to the finale as 'like dying', while a clip of the swan attack from the third Assignment was shown, to the amusement of the studio audience. *Sapphire & Steel* may have completed its run on television long ago, but its influence is still being felt; and alongside the televised Assignments, there are other stories to seek out and enjoy …

APPENDIX A: THE DVDS

The series was first released on DVD by Carlton in August 2002, with two box sets. Unfortunately there were some glitches with the disc authoring on these sets, causing playback problems. In terms of extras, an assortment of text cast biographies, press releases and the like were found on each disc. Better was the box set for the US market released the following year, which included commentaries from P J Hammond and Shaun O'Riordan on the first episode of each of the first two stories, as well as audio introductions for the last four Assignments and the original tape trial of the opening title music. Again, the transfer was not completely satisfactory, with an incorrect frame rate and a 'filmised' look on some episodes. Completists were also left wanting by both box sets removing the advert screen caps from Assignments Three to Six. The latter shortcoming was corrected on the Australian Region 4 release, which also had the best picture quality of the three initial releases.

It was left to Network Video to finally release a more complete box set in 2007: a region 2 release with a quality sound and image transfer, advert screencaps intact and a more extensive set of extras. These extras included: a P J Hammond and Shaun O' Riordan commentary on the first and last episodes of the series; a 30 minute overview documentary; a 20 page booklet by Tim Worthington; script PDFs of Assignment One episode three and Assignment Three episode five; floor plans for four Assignments; PR synopses of all the series; over 360 gallery images; plus PR brochures and flyers. While the documentary was extremely rewarding, its short length necessitated a talking head format with Hammond, O'Riordan, David McCallum and Joanna Lumley taking a breakneck tour through the series' history. On this set, the first episode of the second Assignment was contained on the first disc, which allowed for greater quality but forced viewers to watch a single episode of the second story before having to change discs to watch the remainder. The omission of the theme tune test trial from the Network release was also unfortunate, but this was not only the first high quality unedited release, but also the first release where stories could be watched in a single stream, without being returned to the menu screen after the end of each episode.

APPENDIX B: THE BOOKS

Sapphire & Steel wasn't a series that attracted a great deal of attention from merchandisers. Apart from press releases and the occasional interview or nostalgia piece in a genre magazine, only two printed works have been published on the subject before now. That's not to say that it isn't referenced in a number of compilation books such as *The Golden Age of ITC* or *The Guinness Book of Classic British TV*, both of which contain engaging write-ups of the series. There are also Joanna Lumley's two autobiographies, both of which give a mention of the programme. But in terms of printed works related solely to *Sapphire & Steel*, the following were the only two items:

SAPPHIRE AND STEEL

Writer: P J Hammond
Publisher: Star Books (1979) and Virgin Books (1992)

Overview: An essential purchase for fans of the show, this novelisation of the first Assignment allows us to see the story from a different perspective, but still through P J Hammond's eyes. Recounting the events largely from Rob's point of view - though not in the first person - Hammond strips down the excess of some of the episodes (paring down Lead's appearance almost to the point of non-existence) and gives more of a psychological insight, in particular into Rob's feelings. The two titular agents are represented as impenetrable beings, at no point sharing their inner thoughts with the readers. Also of interest are additional information on some plot elements, and a few slight changes from the televised story. For the former, we get the confirmation that when Rob's 'father' takes him, unseen, through the kitchen, they have travelled back in time three days 'on a mirror-line'. Alterations come with some of the dialogue; and Constable Brian Trelawney becomes Constable Daly in the book. Significant to the continuity of the series as a whole is that the number of elements has been changed. The TV version talked about 127 elements, including 12 Transuranics. Here Sapphire speaks of 'about 127, *not* counting the non-basic elements.' If these 'non-basic' elements were indeed the Transuranics then that would make 'about' 139 in total in the written world of *Sapphire & Steel*. Perhaps the most horrifying change is that Rob's 'mother' from the final episode doesn't just have painted-on eyes in the book, but is instead completely faceless, echoing the Shape from later in the series.

A rare example of a creator-written novelisation, *Sapphire and Steel* was released during the airing of the first Assignment and runs to around 40,000 words, this modest length perhaps indicating it was aimed at the younger end of the market. It is nevertheless very nicely written, though the progression of the series to a more adult concern perhaps indicates why Hammond wasn't asked to write a follow-up. The format was also one that the writer confessed he was not comfortable with.

The novelisation was reissued by Virgin to tie in with the initial video releases in 1992. This second edition came with a new introduction by Hammond.

SAPPHIRE AND STEEL ANNUAL 1981

Publisher: World International Publishing Limited (1980)

Overview: Annuals are traditionally published around the August of the year preceding their cover date, in time to catch the Christmas market, and the sole *Sapphire & Steel* example was no exception – which ironically meant that it appeared in a year when the show hadn't actually been on television. The book was produced by World International, a group that had made its name releasing annuals on a wide variety of television properties, usually containing a mixture of text and comic stories, and peppered with completely unrelated fact and filler features. The *Sapphire and Steel Annual* follows the usual pattern, though in fairness at least articles on telepathy and the *Mary Celeste* are pertinent to the series. A small quiz and the factual story of a man who can make photographs with his mind are both of tenuous interest, though quite what the Bermuda Triangle, UFOs, the 1624 'lost colony', hypnotic regression and black holes have to do with *Sapphire & Steel* is open to debate. The text stories included in the book are nicely written for a young age group and comprise five tales running from five to nine pages each, with monochrome and colour illustrations. What's most notable about the illustrations is that likenesses aren't at a premium; the renditions of Steel tend to resemble David Warner more than they do David McCallum. Also of note is the titular creature in the story 'Rogue Robot', which very closely resembles the eponymous machine seen in the 1974 *Doctor Who* television serial 'Robot'. Although credited to P J Hammond, who had final approval on the content, the book was written and illustrated by staff writers for World International who can no longer be traced. There are instances of time travel in the stories, which bothered Hammond. For example, Sapphire is shown taking time forward a year, but, as with the *Look-In* comic strips on which he was also erroneously credited as writer (see Appendix C), Hammond understood that they were for a younger audience and so raised no major objections towards them. In a 1993 interview with website author Rob Stanley, Hammond noted that both formats 'tended to contradict the premise that had been set in the original TV series, that "time" was only allowed to break into the present day. As both of these publications were geared to younger readers, it did not worry me too much.'

APPENDIX C: THE COMIC STRIPS

The week in which the broadcast of Assignment Two was temporarily shelved due to an ITV strike was also, coincidentally, the week in which the children's comic magazine *Look-In* began running a *Sapphire & Steel* comic strip.

The popular strip ran until May 1980, had a three month break, then returned for another eight months before being discontinued between the TV broadcasts of Assignments Four and Five. Altogether 76 issues containing the strip were produced, with a further text story appearing in the 1981 *Look-In* Annual (again published in 1980, when the series was off the air). For this listing, I have split the strip stories into 'Seasons' based around when the breaks in the publication occurred.

While the strips perhaps understandably focus on the young (all of the stories feature a child as a main character) and there's a certain predilection with the supernatural, they were extremely well crafted for the medium, and would make a very nice collected edition if anyone ever had the mind and resources to do this.

Speaking to TotalSciFi Online in 2007, Hammond reflected: 'I was very fond of the *Look-In* comic strips. I had a fascinating meeting with Arthur Ranson when the project was planned. And he would always send me proofs of the text before each publication. He was so talented and dedicated to the series.'

Note: Each year, *Look-In* would reset the first issue of the year back to number one, explaining the somewhat confusing issue numbering below. Perhaps even more confusing was that the first issue released in each year would actually have a cover date of the final week of the previous year.

SEASON ONE: 11/8/1979 - 3/5/1980

Writer: Angus Allan
Artist: Arthur Ranson
Publisher: Independent Television Publications Ltd

Story One
Issues: 33-40
Dates: 11/8/1979 - 29/9/1979

Summary: Artist Jack Terris lives with his son Marcus in a remote moorland house, where one of his paintings possesses him and tries to trap Marcus, Sapphire and Steel in mirrors.

Overview: A first tale that reads like *Alice in Wonderland* meets *Dr Jekyll and Mr Hyde*, this is a fairly charming opening that manages to prefigure some of the themes in Assignment Four. One of the unfortunate things about British children's comic strips at the time was a tendency toward unnaturalistic, antiquated dialogue, and that's in evidence here, with 'What the Dickens' and 'Jolly good' appearing on the first page alone. This is, however, a small distraction from a story that's mildly outside the series' remit but nevertheless works.

Story Two
Issues: 41-45
Dates: 6/10/1979 - 3/11/1979

Summary: Sarah Johnson, a deaf and mute girl, is celebrating her fourteenth birthday. Unfortunately the necklace and ring she receives as presents from her parents bring forth the possessed spirit of a painting.

Overview: Although this story resembles the previous one in using a 'possessed painting' motif, it has a different take on it, with an understated 'coming of age' subtext. What's most notable is that Steel acts as the empath, sensing the history of an old painting, while Sapphire has the physical role, punching out the face of said painting in order to restore time.

Story Three
Issues: 46-51
Dates: 10/11/1979 - 15/12/1979

Summary: Author David Rochester lives in a lighthouse with his wife and young son Lee. When Lee finds an old ship's anchor it causes a rift in time, through which a French naval officer pulls him back into the past and tries to change history ...

Overview: The first *Sapphire & Steel* story to be based around a lighthouse, pre-empting the Big Finish play (see Appendix D) by 25 years. On the subject of trivia, the look of the author in the story is actually based on the strip's own author, Angus Allan. In a plot clearly inspired by that of the first television story, we have Steel freezing soldiers and an appearance by Lead. The latter character is able to shrink soldiers down to miniscule size, though his image is that of a generic muscular black man, and not specifically a likeness of Val Pringle.

Story Four
Issues: 1-3
Dates: 29/12/1980 - 12/1/1980

Summary: Mr Bernard Smith takes part in a magician's stage act, only to find that an old song and the age of the magician's cabinet take him back in time to ancient Egypt ...

Overview: While far-fetched even by *Sapphire & Steel* standards and possessing an anti-climatic ending, this is one of the most inspired of the comic strips, with some spectacular artwork. One can only imagine the macabre plot P J Hammond could have created using the idea of a magician's cabinet in the series.

Story Five
Issues: 4-6
Dates: 19/1/1980 - 2/2/1980

Summary: Young Diane Simpson lives in a high-rise flat with her parents. Her vivid imagination causes chaos when a pretend cat and a made-up rhyme cause the spirit of Hecate, the greatest witch of ancient times, to take over her body. Sapphire and Steel must bring back Diane before her possessed form destroys the Houses of Parliament.

Overview: As evidenced by the story description, this is one of the most far-fetched stories from the comics, and scarcely within the series' remit. However, possibly because it was the joint shortest strip (along with story seven), it was chosen for reprint in 2007 in the hardback special: *Look-In: The Best of the Seventies* (Carlton Books).

Story Six
Issues: 7-11
Dates: 9/2/1980 - 8/3/1980

Summary: School friends Danny Lewis and Geoff Foster discover that an old military cap badge brings forth a wartime traitor, Captain Simpson, to wreak havoc in the present day.

Overview: This is perhaps the story that most starkly represents the curiously anachronistic style of strip writing of the time. Surely no schoolchild in the country was really saying 'crumbs' and 'jolly' in 1979? It's also amusing to see Sapphire and Steel meet up in a McDonald's fast food outlet for a conference! Steel claims during the story, 'We're not immortal!' - possibly confirmation of series background detail in the strip. However, the notion that the stories are in any way canonical is questionable. Although P J Hammond had approval on all the comic strips, his editorial comments were never that major, as he appreciated that they were aimed at a different audience.

Story Seven

Issues: 12-14
Dates: 15/3/1980 - 29/3/1980

Summary: Anna and Martin Brown are exploring some moorlands when they find a disused railway line and an old belt buckle. The buckle acts as a trigger, taking Anna back to a time when her grandmother died in a railway crash: the same crash that Anna is now about to experience ...

Overview: A competent yet rudimentary instalment in the series, showing that three-issue stories didn't really allow for the development of a full plotline. The revelation that Anna's grandmother was a witch is another nod to the comic series' fascination with the supernatural. But at just six pages it all feels a little too inconsequential.

Story Eight
Issues: 15-19
Dates: 5/4/1980 - 3/5/1980

Summary: Billy Moon is taken back in time by a painting in a junkshop, finding himself in 1666, where Time tries to take him over and kill him.

Overview: One of only three strip stories to reference the date (given here and in story 11 as '1980', and in story 12 as 'December 1980') and also the third story in which a painting acts as a trigger. Nevertheless the first 'season' of *Sapphire & Steel* comic strips was a strong one, even if there are signs in this closing strip - with extensive time travel and demons - that the quality control would soon drop. That turned out to be the case for the second season, where elves, wizards and Satan took turns to appear in ever more outlandish adventures ...

SEASON TWO: 9/8/1980 - 18/4/1981

Story Nine
Issues: 33-37

Dates: 9/8/1980 - 6/9/1980

Summary: Andy Illington is on holiday with his parents when he accidentally discovers a tunnel that leads to Cawdroc, an evil sorcerer from the dark ages.

Overview: The strip returns to *Look-In* after a three month break, and it's with one of the sillier stories. *The Cave of Cawdroc,* where the wizard lies trapped in the Tunnel of Time, is pure hokum that gets by almost by virtue of Allan's superb art alone.

Story Ten
Issues: 38-44
Dates: 13/9/1980 - 25/10/1980

Summary: When protesters clash with construction workers at the site of an old Victorian Mill, the violence calls forth the spirit of a Victorian child, determined to have his revenge for the slavery he endured there.

Overview: The story seems to be alarmingly topical, but actually predates the violent miners' strike of Britain by three years. In one sense, the unusually violent and gritty tone puts it outside the scope of *Sapphire & Steel,* but in another it makes it the best strip *Look-In* ever ran. One particularly notable element of *all* the comic strips is that Sapphire is a far more dominant character than she was initially seen to be on screen, with Steel being almost her passive partner in comparison. This is particularly evident in a scene where Sapphire draws out the hatred of time by beating Steel up …

Story Eleven
Issues: 45-49
Dates: 1/11/1980 - 29/11/1980

Summary: A tribal mask causes Nick Twain to fall through time and into the African jungles of 1890 where his great, great grandfather was an explorer. There, dark forces want him to recreate an ancient battle so that the satanic witch doctor M'Ganga might live …

Overview: While essentially a borderline offensive account of colonialist superstitions, there are occasional lines of dialogue that work against the source. Witness Steel asking of Sapphire, 'Have you stopped to think? Everything that happened when Europeans took over this African Continent wasn't good ...' Also of note is the most disturbing representation of 'Time' in the strip, as an ominous face appearing from trees and branches. Issue 46 marked the sixth and final time that an illustration of Sapphire and Steel would appear on a *Look-In* cover, though the 1980 Annual also included them on the cover and on a photographic poster inside.

Story Twelve
Issues: 50-52, 1-4
Dates: 6/12/1980 - 17/1/1981

Summary: Sapphire and Steel travel back to 1864 to meet Zebediah Clench, an evil sorcerer who has captured two children from 1980 during a theatre production of Dickens' *A Christmas Carol*.

Overview: Though having a Christmas story based around Dickens' play is something of a cliché, *Sapphire & Steel* does it better than most by continuing the preceding story's curious obsession with the Devil. Today, such subject matter seems extremely odd for a child market; but a TV tie-in strip that had such quaint dialogue as 'Confound it!' for Steel also had Beelzebub himself putting in an appearance. Despite the second season of strips by this stage having virtually no resemblance to *Sapphire & Steel* on TV, it's still commendable work.

Story Thirteen
Issues: 5-13
Dates: 24/1/1981 - 21/3/1981

Summary: Tristran and Catherine Pendelton are taken back in time via an old book on Scandinavian folk legends and some pan pipes. They arrive in the land of Gronandyl, an ancient battleground for armies of dwarves and elves. Magisfard, the leader of the elves, plans to use them to make certain his land is never sunk beneath the sea ...

Overview: With nine instalments, this was the longest of the strips presented in *Look-In*. As the summary attests, the strip has by this stage *completely* abandoned any resemblance to the television series, though the artwork is still tremendous. In particular, look out for Ranson experimenting with panels that stretch the full width of the page, something commonplace now, but possibly a first then. However, with Sapphire's physical presence increased - including scenes of her beating up random elves - this is easily the weakest of the run. Also of note is that with Issue 7 the magazine included one of a handful of features on the series, in this case an interview with Joanna Lumley. Particularly memorable is her observation, '[David McCallum]'s a very clever actor. I feel like a fourth former doing the school play opposite the head boy.'

Story Fourteen
Issues: 14-17
Dates: 28/3/1981 - 18/4/1981

Summary: The Pied Piper of Hamelin appears in the present day as Evil Eric, the lead singer of pop group Tarquin. Playing at a Midlands nightclub, he takes all the children present into another dimension, leaving Sapphire and Steel to track him down ...

Overview: Despite the lame premise, there are actually some interesting concepts in this final story. One is that the Pied Piper is a foe that Sapphire and Steel have fought before, as seen in a brief prelude, and who has escaped. In this sense it's rather like what would happen if the Shape from Assignment Four ever broke free. Also of note is that Time has changed history to alter their past actions ... thoughtful ideas for the strip's final bow out, despite the obvious decline in story-telling discipline. Perhaps the greatest indication of how far out of touch the strip had fallen was that Evil Eric's appearance appeared to be closely modelled on that of Johnny Rotten of the punk group the Sex Pistols ... despite the fact that the group had disbanded some three years before the strip came to be published.

Additional #1: 'The Albatross'

Summary: Moving into a new home with his parents, Adam Carter finds an old bosun's whistle. Upon blowing it, he is taken back in time to the sailing ship *The Albatross*, as Time, in the form of a seagull, tries to change military history.

Overview: The last gasp of *Sapphire & Steel* in *Look-In* before Allan and Ranson were reassigned to work on the strip for *Buck Rogers in the 25th Century*. With the initial contract expiring, this was a six-page text story in the 1981 *Look-In Annual*, featuring black and white illustrations from Ranson. Like most of the later strips it's far removed from the television stories, with more time travel involved, but it's a pleasant enough goodbye from the magazine to the series.

Additional #2: 'Party Animals'
Issues: Doctor Who Magazine, #173
Dates: 15/5/1991

Summary: Sapphire and Steel attend a party held by the Dæmon, Banjaxx.

Overview: An indulgent yet fun one-off strip for *Doctor Who Magazine* written by Gary Russell and illustrated by Mike Collins/Steve Pini. Featuring several incarnations of the Doctor at a party, it also has cameos by the likes of Captain Britain, Steed, Death's Head and Bart Simpson. Included here for completeness, as one panel presented a cameo by Sapphire and Steel.

APPENDIX D: THE AUDIO PLAYS

The company Big Finish, best known for producing a range of original *Doctor Who* audio plays, announced in May 2004 they had acquired the licence to release new *Sapphire & Steel* stories. A long hold-up with various negotiations and red tape followed, leading co-producer Nigel Fairs to recall: 'The headaches for *Sapphire & Steel* were more like migraines.'

After a wait of a year, the first season of five stories was finally released, with David Warner and Susannah Harker taking the lead roles after McCallum and Lumley declined to return. David Collings reprised his role as Silver in two of the stories, while Mark Gatiss performed that of Gold. Popular *Doctor Who* actors such as Colin Baker and Richard Franklin appeared throughout both this season and the second, which followed six months later, this time consisting of six stories. Lisa Bowerman played Ruby in this season. After a ten month break, a third and possibly final season was released, once more featuring David Collings as Silver and with a guest role in the fourth story for another *Doctor Who* actress, Louise Jameson.

It should be noted that the audios were aimed largely at a new audience rather than at those seeking a nostalgic look back. How such a strategy is received is down to personal taste, though as this book is chiefly a look at *Sapphire & Steel* as a television series, then it's fair to note that there are some significant differences between the two. Surprisingly, the change of leads is actually the least concern. More controversial is that many of the stories, somewhat out of kilter with the ethos of the original show, feature profanity, sexual content and implied graphic violence.

Note: In the following discussion of the audio stories, plot elements are frequently revealed, perhaps making it preferable for the reader to have heard them first.

SEASON ONE

Cast: David Warner (Steel) and Susannah Harker (Sapphire)
Crew: Toby Robinson (Recording), Nigel Fairs (Post-production and Music), David Darlington (CD Mastering), Cyril Ornadel (Series Theme), David Darlington/Steve Foxon (Theme Remastering), P J Hammond (Original Series Creator), Granda Ventures Ltd (Licence Providers), Andrew Orton (Cover and Packaging Design), Lisa Bowerman (Photography), John Ainsworth (Website), Brenda Smith/Chris Eaton (Big Finish Administration) and Jason Haigh-Ellery/Nigel Fairs (Producers). Recorded at The Moat Studios.

Story One: The Passenger
Writer: Steve Lyons
Director: Jason Haigh-Ellery
Production: The second story of the first block, recorded in August 2004
Release Date: May 2005
Duration: Four Episodes – 29′ 03″/29′ 11″/27′ 12″/27′ 33″
Additional Cast: Mark Gatiss (Gold), Hugo Myatt (Philip Burgess), Jackie Skarvellis (Mrs Warburton), Neil Henry (John Andrews) and Clare Louise Connelly (The Princess).

Summary: Sapphire and Steel arrive in a train constructed sometime between 1932 and 1934 … yet time doesn't exist outside and each carriage has a different time zone ranging from 1919 to 2004. The only passenger on the train is Phillip Burgess, a 66-year-old antiquarian book dealer from the present day. Burgess has a novel with him that, although unnamed, is clearly Agatha Christie's *Murder on the Orient Express*, and this acts as a trigger for Time to convert the dead passengers to act as characters from the book.

Time uses the guilt of Burgess – 15 years earlier he was a train driver who crashed his train, causing the death of a young girl passenger – to transfer to the other passengers, making them believe they were killed by Burgess and converting them into 12 would-be murderers, with Burgess as their target. Sapphire, Steel and Gold are all that stand between the 12 passengers and Burgess's murder, while the enemy – in the form of a faceless conductor – manipulates them all ...

Overview:
Along with 'All Fall Down' and 'Remember Me', 'The Passenger' is the audio play to most resemble the original television series. Likeable and charming, it nevertheless feels like a pastiche of both drama conventions and the series itself. Many of the staple ingredients of the series, including children's rhymes and multiple time zones, are reused, and the situation is populated with character parodies. The scenario is reminiscent of Assignment Five, in that it has somewhat clichéd guest roles in an Agatha Christie homage, and the dialogue also tends to be frequently overwritten. Whereas Hugo Myatt engages as Mr Burgess and Clare Louise Connelly is stunning in the role of a child, Jackie Skarvellis's Mrs Warburton is weighed down by exposition, causing the character to veer towards send-up. Despite all this, and the somewhat one-dimensional Gold, Warner and Harker are both strong in creating a subtly different take on the lead characters.

Story Two: Daisy Chain
Writer: Joseph Lidster
Director: Nigel Fairs
Production: The first story of the first block, recorded in August 2004
Release Date: July 2005
Duration: Four Episodes – 22' 37"/17' 14"/18' 31"/24' 59"
Additional Cast: Kim Hartman (Gabrielle), Lena Rae (Jennifer), Stuart Piper (James), Saul Jaffe (Voice), Emma Kilbey (Voice) and Joseph Lidster (Tom).

Summary: Sapphire and Steel are assigned to a suburban household, where James Sowersby has come home from University to his mother Gabrielle and his teenage sister Jennifer. Yet behind the doors of number 29 lurks the spirit of Joshua, the stillborn twin of Jennifer. Possessing a music box where its ashes are stored, the spirit terrorises the family, using television and telepathy, and electrocutes a pizza delivery man. The music box - an old family heirloom - and Jennifer's grief cause Joshua's spirit to grow in strength, a situation that only Jennifer can resolve …

Trivia: Although not revealed in the story itself or on the CD packaging, the setting for this play is 2004, as noted on the Big Finish website. Sapphire's powers are hugely increased from what we saw on screen, as she takes back the entire lives of a family. Writer Joseph Lidster observed: 'I found, when watching the series, that their powers seemed quite vague, and I do think, especially in something like *Sapphire & Steel*, that such things shouldn't restrict the story.' A behind-the-scenes featurette lasting 14' 01" is included on the first disc.

Overview:
One of the more interesting Big Finish audio plays, 'Daisy Chain' is a very experimental and very modern take on the series. Having the ghost of a child controlling television is a very fresh idea, and there are touches of post-modernism as the theme music gets 'switched over' as if the story itself is just another programme on the airwaves. There's also an interesting alteration in the roles of Sapphire and Steel as detectives. The family already know, at least on an unconscious level, what is behind the disturbances, so it's up to the two agents to coerce the truth out of them, rather than piece clues together. Sadly, however, the youthful voice of many of the Big Finish writers can distract when contrasted with Hammond's, and the guest cast are a little self-conscious. The final resolution - Sapphire passes a young girl a piece of broken glass so she can slash her own wrists, then leaves her family to find her dead body - is repugnant. As a result, the play is one likely to polarise listeners, though Lidster justified the choice of ending: 'I really don't think it's any darker than Tully's death in the TV series. He doesn't even have a choice - Steel murders him. Jen does have a choice … "Daisy Chain" is a horror story but with what I feel is a genuine emotional core. It needed a strong ending, and I stand by Jen's death as being

the strongest ending it could have had.'

Story Three: All Fall Down
Writer: David Bishop
Director: Nigel Fairs
Production: The first story of the second block, recorded in February 2005
Release Date: August 2005
Duration: Four Episodes – 22' 07"/28' 14"/25' 51"/30' 38"
Additional Cast: David Collings (Silver), Michael Chance (Webber), Kate Dyson (Flemming), Suzanne Proctor (Mary), Linda Bartram (The Girl) and Neil Cole (Policeman).
Additional Crew: Andrew Aitchison (Photography, with Lisa Bowerman),

Summary: Sapphire and Steel arrive at an historical archives building in present day London. While there, they discover Silver has arrived before them, and that Sapphire's voice has been recorded on an old phonograph from 1892. Investigating via the anomaly of time bubbles, they meet Weyburn, a German inventor who took photographs of the insane in the belief that this would cure them. Steel is struck down with symptoms of the plague, while Sapphire and Silver discover that the archives building was built on the site of plague deaths.

With Steel's health worsening and Silver unable to find a way back to the present, Sapphire is trapped in 1892, with a Dr Webber who was imprisoned there in perpetuity in a timeloop by Maldeb, his imaginary friend given life. Webber sent out 'shards of time' to draw Sapphire towards him. But before Sapphire can rescue anyone, she has to contend with the mysterious Maldeb …

Trivia: Several proposed scenes – including Webber threatening to burn himself alive and a smoking corpse – were removed as it was decided they would not work in the audio-only medium.

David Collings, the only actor to reprise a role from the original TV series, praised the performances of both his new co-stars: 'David [Warner]'s wonderful; they both are. I don't think he's as taciturn [as Steel] as David [McCallum] was. They're all different people.'

Though Silver spends much of his time with Sapphire in this story, Collings met only Warner during recording of this first audio, and only Harker for 'Dead Man Walking'. A third story for the third season was recorded by Collings in a day without either star being present: 'You're all in separate recording booths, and if the other person's not there, you just have someone read the lines, and you just sort of have to act round it. It's done terribly quickly, there's no time for getting it wrong, you just have to go off the page in one take if possible; you're sort of working against the clock all the time.'

'Maldeb' is a reverse spelling of 'Bedlam', the name associated with a 16th Century hospital for the insane.

Overview:
'All Fall Down' should probably be the first port of call for anyone coming to the audios as a fan of the television series. Not only does it adhere to the family-friendly tone of the television episodes, but it's the one that most feels like it could be a story from that medium. This is helped in large part by David Collings reprising his role as Silver. While the character was arguably ambiguous in the series, it's revealed (in 'Cruel Immortality') that Silver was the one who released Sapphire and Steel from the café, which explains the rather more placid, 'loveable uncle' persona he adopts here. It also makes a difference that Collings is, of course, significantly older, rendering the character less edgy by default. As for the leads, Warner spends much of the final episode absent, struck down by the plague that imperils the characters of the story. A major disadvantage faced by the season one writers was that they had yet to hear the roles as played by Harker and Warner. As writer David Bishop admitted, 'At the time I was writing "All Fall Down", I had no idea who would be playing Sapphire or Steel, so it was helpful knowing exactly what the voice of Silver would sound like. For the two leads, I watched my DVDs of the TV stories and tried to write the characters as if they were being played by Lumley and McCallum.' If there's any flaw with 'All Fall Down', it's that it lacks the claustrophobic atmosphere of the best television stories, and is slightly more science fiction orientated than usual. But nevertheless this is an engaging and respectful homage to the programme.

Story Four: The Lighthouse
Writer: Nigel Fairs
Director: John Ainsworth
Production: The final story of the first block, recorded in August 2004
Release Date: November 2005
Duration: Two Episodes – 32′ 52″/33′ 58″
Additional Cast: Neil Salvage (Old Man), Joseph Young (Adrian), Ian Hallard (Nicholas), Lucy Beresford (Suzy), Michael Adams (Mike) and Stuart Piper (Young Boy).

Summary: Sapphire and Steel are investigating the events of Penryth Point Lighthouse, a building that dates back to 1858. The lighthouse is occupied in 2004 by Nicholas, a homophobic mass murderer, who likes to sketch nude men prior to killing them, reacting against his own homosexual nature. Time is disrupted when the killer as a young man arrives at the lighthouse with his wife in 1972.

The agents get caught up in the time storm as both eras collide, and get thrown outside of time. Nicholas is driven mad in 1972 by denying his own nature and love for his friend Adrian. His self hatred causes him to kill his wife and embark on his murder spree. Steel realises that the trigger causing the time storm is not only a painting but also the knife that Nicholas uses to kill himself as an old man. There is too much blood on it, and it's only when Steel convinces the older Nicholas to kill himself with a gun that time is put back on the right track.

Overview:
'Daisy Chain' had already featured one or two instances of very minor profanity, but here Nigel Fairs takes *Sapphire & Steel* by the scruff of the neck and throws the quaint little show into a world of four-letter abuse, pornography and homophobic murderers. How much the play can be enjoyed depends on personal taste; how much it can be regarded as a *Sapphire & Steel* story even more so. The script is innovative in structure, having a cyclical nature that contains separate plot strands from three different time zones. However, in many senses it goes against the nature of the series, in that like many of the other audio plays it features movement

through time – Time breaking out – rather than Time breaking in. Another cause of concern is that the two titular agents are largely passive observers, their role almost rudimentary, and the resolution again takes the form of one of them encouraging a suicide. These qualms aside, 'The Lighthouse' is a well produced story with some striking performances. As Fairs observed, 'With *Sapphire & Steel*, we agreed from very early on that we would try to "push the limits". P J Hammond didn't limit himself with the television series, so I think it's fitting that we don't either.'

Story Five: Dead Man Walking
Writer: Nigel Fairs
Director: John Ainsworth
Production: The final story of the second block, recorded in February 2005
Release Date: January 2006
Duration: Two Episodes – 34' 28"/26' 09"
Additional Cast: David Collings (Silver), Arthur Bostrom (Richard Hanmore), Trevor Littledale (Michael Kent), Jo Castleton (Marian Anderson), Neil Cole (Ian Jackson), Michael Chance (Hammond), Nigel Fairs (Kilsby), Suzanne Proctor (Marcus), and Linda Bartram (Mo).
Additional Crew: Steve Foxon (Post-Production and Music in place of Nigel Fairs; CD Mastering in place of David Darlington)

Summary: Sapphire and Steel investigate Blackledge Prison, where an inmate has committed suicide in an empty cell. While exploring the cell alone, Steel finds himself transported back to 1968 in the body of one Michael Kent, a child murderer. Meanwhile, back in 2004, Sapphire is joined by Silver, and they both meet a second Michael Kent. It's left to the agents to restore the fractures in time, and work out just what part Officer Jackson had to play in events.

Trivia: 'Dead Man Walking' was devised and due to be written by John Ainsworth. Ainsworth wrote around a page of story ideas, but as Nigel Fairs noted: '[John] didn't have time to write the actual script, so I stepped in and scribbled it at the last moment.' A music suite lasting 4' 57" is included as the thirteenth track of the disc, while a 54 minute 'Big Finish Sample Disc' was also included.

Overview:
Nigel Fairs wasn't enamoured of his own script, noting, 'Though I think it's a great idea, and I think Steve did a fabulous job on the sound design, it's probably one of my least favourites, to be honest. It was all rather rushed, as I remember, and a bit of a mess.' It's perhaps an unfair assessment, given that 'Dead Man Walking' has a lot of story to tell in a single hour, including another appearance by Silver, and consequently rewards repeat listens. As with 'The Lighthouse', there are plenty of expletives in the play, perhaps distancing purists, though unlike 'The Lighthouse' the story doesn't really work in the single disc format. Subsequently the idea of having stories on one disc was scrapped for the series, leaving the often muddled narrative of 'Dead Man Walking' one of the casualties of the experiment. It is also a concern that the emotional peak of the drama is mishandled by a guest cast, who perhaps lacked the necessary experience to carry off such a dark and brutal scenario. However, David Collings, reprising the Silver role, commented: 'I think possibly the stories made more sense in the audio ones, the writers took the characters and put them into situations, and it was sort of altered, somewhat. Not quite the same; they were more logical, the stories. The stories make some sort of sense, which didn't seem to be a problem on television, we didn't worry about that.' In all, 'Dead Man Walking' is an interesting albeit flawed experiment.

SEASON TWO

Cast: David Warner (Steel) and Susannah Harker (Sapphire)
Crew: Toby Robinson (Recording), Cyril Ornadel (Series Theme), David Darlington/Steve Foxon (Theme Remastering), P J Hammond (Original Series Creator), Andrew Orton (Logo Design), John Ainsworth (Website), Brenda Smith/Chris Eaton (Big Finish Administration) and Jason Haigh-Ellery/Nigel Fairs (Producers). Recorded at The Moat Studios.

Story Six: The School
Writer: Simon Guerrier

Director: Nigel Fairs
Production: The second story of the first block, recorded in February 2006
Release Date: July 2006
Duration: Four Episodes - 20′ 09″/19′ 08″/21′ 22″/23′ 09″
Additional Cast: Keith Drinkel (Mr Leslie), Lisa Daniely (Mrs Leslie), Victoria Gould (Chatura) and James Daniel Wilson (Max).
Additional Crew: Alistair Lock (Post-production and Music), David Darlington (CD Mastering), William Johnston (Dialogue Edit), Lee Binding (Cover and Packaging Design) and Lisa Bowerman (Photography).

Summary: Sapphire and Steel investigate a 100-year-old school where children haunt the teachers. The presence of the school takes over the agents, causing them to regress mentally to childhood. After they manage to escape the walls of ghosts that inhabit the building, they discover that the entire school is an illusion, conjured up by a Mrs Leslie, desperate for her deceased husband to return. Time had offered a chance for the two teachers to be reunited, but the memories of the school had also flooded 'Mr Leslie''s mind, meaning he could never be the man he was. Realising this, Mrs Leslie lets the illusion fade away, and Sapphire and Steel leave her to her tears.

Trivia: A 14′ 07″ behind-the-scenes featurette is included on the first disc.

Overview:
Although the second season audio plays are more traditional and drop elements like the bad language, the first three are still likely to split opinion for various different reasons. With 'The School', that reason is that the final episode sees the two agents become children. Ultimately such an excursion means that the story cannot be objectively regarded as a success or a failure; the listener either likes Harker and Warner saying such lines as 'Steel is a lame-o, Steel is a lame-o', or not. While Warner is frequently hilarious in this new persona, it's a world away from the claustrophobic trappings of previous stories, and the move towards quirkiness over scares does harm the production somewhat. However, one notable element is

that with Alistair Lock taking over the role of musician the likeable incidentals veer towards a percussive, retro sound that are almost a homage to the work of Cyril Ornadel. It's this that helps 'The School' to feel more in keeping with the programme's ethos, despite the fact that, with the offbeat subject matter and Steel assaulting various characters, including Sapphire, it's still quite a way removed.

Story Seven: The Surest Poison
Writer: Richard Dinnick
Director: Nigel Fairs
Production: The first story of the first block, recorded in February 2006
Release Date: September 2006
Duration: Four Episodes – 27' 18"/29' 53"/14' 45"/14' 07"
Additional Cast: Richard Franklin (Mr Webb), Tom Bevan (Abraham Louis Breguet), Eric MaClennan (Gerrard DuBourg) and Helen Goldwyn (Cecile).
Additional Crew: Steve Foxon (Post-production and Music), David Darlington (CD Mastering), Lee Binding (Cover and Packaging Design) and Lisa Bowerman (Photography).

Summary: Sapphire and Steel investigate a collection of antique watches that lead through cracks in time. Their journeys take them from present day England to Paris of 1795 and Jerusalem of 1983 … and dealings with an auctioneer who has been cursed with immortality.

Trivia: A behind-the-scenes look at 'The Lighthouse' is included on the second disc, lasting 19' 57".

Overview:
'The Surest Poison' is an intricate story that takes place in multiple timelines, with a number of situations to command the attention. In fact, what is heard on the finished audio is actually simplified from the original script, a subplot with the auctioneer in 18th Century Paris having been removed for clarity. This explains the somewhat disparate lengths of the episodes. While the play is very carefully written and researched (it references real historical accounts), the

reason why it is grouped in with 'The School' and 'Water Like a Stone' as one that may divide listeners is that it contains English actors speaking with French accents. The acceptance or otherwise of such an element is entirely down to the ear of the listener. Indeed, the release received a disparaging review in the cult magazine *SFX*, something that writer Richard Dinnick put down as, '*SFX* were – at best – being unkind.' The story also involves extensive time travel, which reverses the concept of the series somewhat. Producer/director Nigel Fairs noted: 'David Warner and I chatted about the possibility of more time travel, and setting things in historical periods. I'm very much in favour of this (I originally intended to set several stories in the past and future), though I realise it strays a little from the original series.'

Story Eight: Water Like A Stone
Writer: Nigel Fairs
Director: John Ainsworth
Production: The first story of the second block, recorded in August 2006
Release Date: November 2006
Duration: Four Episodes – 20' 29"/28' 03"/20' 43"/20' 12"
Additional Cast: Lisa Bowerman (Ruby), Nicholas Briggs (Arthur Bunnings), Lucy Gaskell (The Girl) and Suzanne Proctor (Dolly).
Additional Crew: Nigel Fairs (Post-production and Music), David Darlington (CD Mastering), Lee Binding (Cover and Packaging Design) and Lisa Bowerman (Photography).

Summary: Sapphire and Steel arrive at the Capital Palace Theatre to investigate disturbances in time with theatre director Arthur Bunnings. In an attempt to impress Steel, fellow agent Ruby opens up a fissure between reality and fiction and temporarily becomes part of *Great Expectations*. Unfortunately, opening up the fissure causes Sapphire and Steel to be dragged into the texts of plays, becoming fictional characters in *The Flood* (a fictional play) and *Cinderella*. Ruby helps to bring them out of the fiction, but then enters it herself. While Ruby remains inside all the plays that have been performed in the theatre, Sapphire and Steel discover the original cause behind the time disturbances: a 17 year old girl, Louisa, who died on the way to the theatre to meet her boyfriend.

Her ghost haunts the building, but agrees to leave after the two agents convince her to accept her death. With the passing of Louisa, the theatre is free of the presence of time manipulation ... but unfortunately this leaves Ruby trapped forever in the fiction of the place.

Trivia: The unnamed song sung by Suzanne Proctor can be heard eight times throughout the play. Its writer, Nigel Fairs, recalled: 'I never gave it an official name, I'm afraid! Suzanne and I referred to it as the "Poor Little Dolly" song, so I guess that's as good a title as any! It was meant to be a nightmare version of the well-known "Waiting by the Church" music hall song, and was intended to really irritate the listener, to the extent that they felt as trapped as Steel and Sapphire were!!'
Outtakes and full songs, lasting 10′ 31″, are included on the second disc.

Overview:
'Water Like a Stone' is a *Sapphire & Steel* Christmas story, set in an old musical theatre on Christmas Eve. While there's the return of mild expletives to the range, for the first half of the production it's a very standard set up. However, from episode three onwards, the story becomes a musical, with multiple renditions of a music hall pastiche song that will doubtless stick in listeners' heads long after the discs have finished playing. With the two agents taking part in seasonal performances, we also have the quirky development of Sapphire and Steel coming out with *double entendres*. Perhaps less effective are the notion of the agents turning into fiction - not an especially original idea - and the new character Ruby, who, like Gold before her, is a little too artificially contrived to accept in the same way as a Silver or even a Lead. Nevertheless, as a production, 'Water Like a Stone' is impressive, with Suzanne Proctor (her third appearance in the range) being particularly notable as the music hall performer, Dolly. Whether a musical *Sapphire & Steel* with little narrative tension is what the series required is, of course, for the listener to judge, but perhaps the only really regrettable thing is that Warner and Harker didn't join in with the songs.

Story Nine: Cruel Immortality

Writer: Nigel Fairs
Director: Lisa Bowerman
Production: The second story of the second block, recorded in August 2006
Release Date: February 2007
Duration: Four Episodes - 26' 23"/24' 49"/25' 50"/23' 31"
Additional Cast: Daphne Oxenford (Enid), Muriel Pavlow (Mrs P), Ian Burford (Stanley), Lois Baxter (Matron) and Steven Kynman/Lucy Gaskell/Lisa Bowerman/Nigel Fairs (Carers).
Additional Crew: Alistair Lock (Post-production and Music), David Darlington (CD Mastering), William Johnston (Wireless Music) and Lee Binding (Cover and Packaging Design).

Summary: After the events of the previous story, Steel has ended his working relationship with Sapphire, believing her too emotionally involved. He finds himself in a nursing home in 1949, tired and forgetful as he begins to become human. The home is populated by sadistic 'carers', the tortured elderly and a dominating matron. Eventually Steel pieces together the truth - the nursing home is another prison devised by the transient beings, who have trapped Sapphire in the body of a bestial version of herself, and given her a mirror image that is an aged resident. The 'carers' are people tricked by the transient beings into believing immortality is a gift, the elderly their own reflections. As Steel finds himself also becoming bestial and an ancient man who forgets why he's there, there seems no way out. Fortunately Sapphire has carved one of the transdimensional chess sets. She then uses the reality-bending nature of the trap to restore Ruby and let her use the chess set to free them in turn.

Trivia: The directing debut of Lisa Bowerman on the range. Bowerman also reprises her role as Ruby, but due to the spoilerish nature of this revelation, it's not included in the credits.
The ninth story was originally due to be 'Big Fun' by Gary Russell, and feature *Doctor Who* actor Colin Baker in a fairground. Unfortunately Russell resigned from Big Finish before this could be realised and the story was subsequently shelved. Nigel Fairs had to write 'Cruel Immortality' as a replacement in two weeks.

Overview:
Arguably the best of the Big Finish *Sapphire & Steel* stories, 'Cruel Immortality' begins with the inevitable experiment in partnership fiction: the solo story. For the first two episodes of the play, Steel is alone in the nursing home, with only a resident, Mrs P – Sapphire in another form – to keep him company. Concerned with his own mortality, Steel becomes an old, embittered man, losing his memory and his purpose. Those who believe that 'less is more' in terms of the mystery of *Sapphire & Steel* may be a little startled by the most revelation-packed story in either television or audio medium. Here we get confirmation that the agents definitely aren't human, that they're immortal and that they don't sleep (something only Steel previously claimed). We also get an oblique yet direct confirmation that it was Silver that rescued them from the café where they were trapped in the final television story. Significantly, Steel confirms that his and Sapphire's relationship is 'business only', a decision Nigel Fairs holds as a progression: 'I think there's a new chemistry. It's a kind of deep loyalty and dependence that personally I find far more interesting than a romantic relationship! If anything I think it's grown from the TV series (if, of course, we're assuming that they're the same Sapphire and Steel!). As for Steel, I'm not convinced that he always tells the truth. Or at the very least, maybe he sometimes lies to himself!'

Story Ten: Perfect Day
Writer: Steve Lyons
Director: Lisa Bowerman
Production: The first story of the third block, recorded in December 2006
Release Date: April 2007
Duration: Four Episodes – 29' 52"/28' 45"/28 57"/30 38"
Additional Cast: Mark Gatiss (Gold), Philip McGough (The Captain), Victoria Carling (Lydia), Daniel Weyman (Richard), Matthew Steer (James) and Caroline Morris (Jen).
Additional Crew: Steve Foxon (Post-production, Music and CD Mastering) and Lee Binding (Cover and Packaging Design).

Summary: A splinter of Time gets on board the yacht *The Perfect Day*, offering the family aboard a chance for a unique kind of immortality. With her daughter due to miscarry and an even worse fate awaiting herself, Lydia Holloway agrees to let Time take them all into a never-ending time bubble, there to relive her daughter's wedding day for eternity. Sapphire, Steel and Gold arrive on board the yacht in order to control the ripples of time, but to do so means destroying the replica ship in a bottle that's controlling the disturbance ... and that will free the splinter to wreak even more havoc.

Overview:
An enjoyable second story from Steve Lyons, reintroducing Gold from his earlier 'The Passenger'. While Lyons' characters aren't perhaps as fully rounded as others in the series, 'Perfect Day' is an improvement over his earlier work, and contains some moments of resolution that are quite ingenuous. The actual plot itself isn't particularly original, the concept of a voyage taking place in a time loop something notably covered in the *Doctor Who Magazine* comic strip *Ship of Fools* in 1980 and the *Doctor Who* TV story 'Carnival of Monsters' back in 1973. Yet Lyons makes full use of the concept, implementing some intriguing plot twists and instilling all his characters with a fear of their own personal futures. Yet despite all of this, and Lisa Bowerman proving to be one of the better directors of the range, the somewhat pedestrian script and lack of narrative tension can cause the story to feel a little flat in places. With the television series, *Sapphire & Steel* was often about what *wasn't* said, and all the associated nuances. Perhaps understandably, due to the format, many of the Big Finish audios tend more towards verbalisation of motif, and 'Perfect Day' indulges in this more than most.

Story Eleven: The Mystery of the Missing Hour
Writer: Joseph Lidster
Director: Nigel Fairs
Production: The second story of the third block, recorded in December 2006
Release Date: June 2007
Duration: Three Episodes – 31′ 58″/37′ 28″/68′ 43″
Additional Cast: Colin Baker (Narrator), Sarah Douglas (Majorie),

Ian Brooker (Cornelius), Cate Debenham-Taylor (Jane/Betty), Ian Hallard (Arthur/Frederick) and Nigel Fairs (MC).
Additional Crew: Nigel Fairs (Post-production and Music), Linda Bartram (vocals), Nicholas Worskett (Solo pianist), David Darlington (CD Mastering) and Simon Holub (Cover and Packaging Design).

Note: The credit for 'David Darlington/Steve Foxon (Theme Remastering)' does not apply to this release, as the story uses a pastiche of the usual theme.

Summary: Amateur detectives Shuffle and Sixpence find themselves in 1926 Cairo investigating how a murder could take place when the suspect had already died - the mystery of the missing hour. Piecing together clues about the case, Mark Shuffle eventually realises that none of it is real, and that his true identity is Steel. He alerts everyone to this fact, including Sixpence - really Sapphire - and the reality breaks down, leaving them part of a recording in a Big Finish studio, 2007. There they discover that Stephen Bunnings, the father of Arthur Bunnings from 'Water Like a Stone', has done a deal with Time in order to achieve immortality in his work. When Stephen rejects the deal, he is returned to reality, leaving Sapphire and Steel trapped on a compact disc that will cause them to cease to exist when it stops playing ...

Trivia: Sarah Douglas is most famous for her role as Ursa in *Superman* and *Superman II,* a fact mentioned in the audio.

Overview:
Another of the second season's quirky, experimental tales, this time an Agatha Christie pastiche with the two leads recast as 'Shuffle' and 'Sixpence'. Colin Baker narrates the story of himself as a young man meeting up with the two 'amateur detectives' in 1926 Egypt, a light, frothy tale that also includes *Sapphire & Steel*'s first sex scene. The story makes use of the comic rapport that Warner and Harker have built up over their time together, there are plenty of witty moments and, as with Lidster's first story, post-modern takes on the nature of the series itself. However, as with any project of this kind, its appeal is a matter of personal taste; a lounge jazz version of the

suicide song from 'Daisy Chain' is either amusingly witty or indulgent, possibly both at the same time. On the same lines, having the supporting characters as deliberate ciphers does limit audience involvement, while the flippancy of the piece deprives the story of dramatic thrust. However, such concerns are turned on their head by the wildly experimental second disc, which features the cast as themselves and Sapphire and Steel trapped on the CD, facing their own destruction. While inventive, the audio tricks used here feel familiar, and the concept of (audio) fourth-wall breaking and format defying does have a certain feeling of 'old hat' attached to it, particularly as it's something that has been tried before on more than one occasion in this very range.

SEASON THREE

Cast: David Warner (Steel) and Susannah Harker (Sapphire)
Crew: Toby Robinson (Recording), Nigel Fairs (Post-Production and Music), David Darlington (CD Mastering), Cyril Ornadel (Series Theme), P J Hammond (Original Series Creator), Simon Holub (Covers & Packaging), Andrew Orton (Logo Design) and Jason Haigh-Ellery/Nigel Fairs (Producers). Recorded at The Moat Studios.

Story Twelve: Second Sight
Writer: Nigel Fairs
Director: Nigel Fairs
Production: Recorded December 2007
Release Date: April 2008
Duration: Four Episodes - 27' 43"/25' 54"/20' 45"/18' 27"
Additional Cast: Blair McDonough (Steel), Anna Skellern (Sapphire), Patience Tomlinson (Mary), Lisa Bowerman (Ruby), Clare Calbraith (Polly), Duncan MacInnes (Davey) and Angela Bruce (Annie).
Additional Crew: John Ainsworth (Website) and Brenda Smith/Chris Eaton (Big Finish Administration)

Summary: The war with the transient beings is spiralling out of control, and Sapphire and Steel learn that Silver has been trapped in a Moebius strip. Even more problematic is the fact that they're now both investigating cases as a pair of Australians, while their real selves are trapped behind a fissure of realities on compact discs. It's left to Ruby to try to restore the real Sapphire and Steel before they're lost forever ...

Trivia: The opening story for Season Three was due to be 'Reborn' by Joseph Lidster, picking up the outstanding plot elements from 'The Mystery of the Missing Hour'. However, Lidster's work schedule meant that a week before recording was due to begin he had still completed only one episode. Nigel Fairs made the decision to write an entirely new story from scratch, inspired by the first television Assignment and with two new actors temporarily taking over the lead roles. Due to this, David Warner and Susannah Harker are listed on the CD packaging as making 'Guest Appearances'.

A behind-the-scenes look at the story is included on the second disc, lasting 5′ 50″.

Overview:
'Second Sight' manages to be a satisfactory audio story despite having several things working against it. Not only was it written within a 33 hour period as an extremely late replacement, but it's also forced to pick up on the plot elements left hanging from the previous story. Perhaps it would have been easier to have Sapphire and Steel immediately released from their CD prison and continuing with a new Assignment, but instead 'Second Sight' features a range of characters that have only tenuous links with the narrative. In particular there's Patience Tomlinson's Mary, a real person placed by the transient beings into a radio play in order to stop Sapphire and Steel escaping. While this is a reasonable development within the structure of the piece, a great deal of the runtime is made up of Mary's monologues, which, while nicely written, have no bearing on the narrative development. Other issues include somewhat clichéd Australian dialogue and a shockingly stereotyped Jamaican house cleaner played by Angela Bruce. Despite this, the script is pleasingly playful, at times lightly parodying the first television story, with dialogue from Sapphire and Steel inversed. There are also some in-jokes, such as one of the characters derisively describing the Big Finish *Tomorrow People*

range as 'sci-fi rubbish'. While 'Second Sight' can't help but feel a little like a plot necessity expanded to 90 minutes, it succeeds in being engaging throughout, if inessential.

Story Thirteen: Remember Me
Writer: John Dorney
Director: Lisa Bowerman
Production: February 2008
Release Date: May 2008
Duration: Four Episodes - 29' 39"/30' 58"/31' 01"/31' 52"
Additional Cast: Sam Kelly (Eric), Joannah Tincey (Kate) and David Horovitch (Nostalgia).
Additional Crew: John Ainsworth (Website) and Brenda Smith/Chris Eaton (Big Finish Administration)

Summary: Eric Gurney is being filmed at a seaside pier for a documentary. A 67-year-old comedian and comedy actor with a faded career, he finds himself trapped with a television crewwoman in a world of his own memories. Under the control of a creature that devours experiences, he finds that Sapphire and Steel are drawn in with him, the creature wanting to feed on their memories too …

Trivia: With a total duration of 123' 30", 'Remember Me' is the longest of Big Finish's *Sapphire & Steel* audio plays.

Overview:
'Remember Me' is a return to traditional storytelling, making it arguably the most authentic Big Finish production in terms of paying homage to the television series. A nice set of scripts by John Dorney uses familiar tropes - an embittered, washed-up entertainer, a deserted seaside setting - and previous *Sapphire & Steel* concepts, yet works them into a fresh and involving landscape. In particular, the idea of a creature that can take memories is a strong one, leaving the two agents unsure as to how many times they've tried to defeat it and whether they actually have done so or are simply recalling planted false memories of their success. It's a treat for purists as it contains such an old-hat mentality that extramarital affairs are referred to as 'opportunities' and the memory of a cinema experience conjures up going to see *Casablanca*. The experience of

the cast also helps the production greatly. Sam Kelly has been performing on television since the 1970s and has had extensive roles in comedies such as *Porridge* (1974-1977), *'Allo, 'Allo* (1982-1991), *On the Up* (1990-1992) and *Barbara* (1995-2003). David Horovitch is also an experienced theatre actor who has worked with the RSC and has extensive television credits, including working with Joanna Lumley in an episode of *The New Avengers*. ('The Last of the Cybernauts ...?', 1976). His other television work includes *Hold The Back Page* (1985-1986), in which he co-starred with David Warner, and *Heat of the Sun* (1998), which also featured Susannah Harker. Along with stories like 'All Fall Down', 'Remember Me' is an ideal starting point for those who have the television series as their first *Sapphire & Steel* experience.

Story Fourteen: Zero
Writer: Steve Lyons
Director: Lisa Bowerman
Production: December 2007
Release Date: June 2008
Duration: Four Episodes – 27′ 56″/27′ 51″/27′ 38″/31′ 11″
Additional Cast: David Collings (Silver), Mark Gatiss (Gold) and Angela Bruce (Andrea).
Additional Crew: Paul Wilson (Website), Brenda Smith/Gary Atterton (Big Finish Administration) and Frances Welsh (Producers' Assistant).

Summary: The war with the transient beings continues amid rumours that they're about to strike *en masse* against the elements, and Copper is missing, possibly having defected. Meanwhile, Silver, having only recently escaped a transient trap, is assigned to a mission with Gold. Together they must investigate a time break on board the space shuttle before its orbit decays, though the mysterious deaths of the crew complicate their mission. When Silver calls in Sapphire and Steel for assistance, Gold's loyalties are thrown into question ...

Trivia: 'Zero' is the second *Sapphire & Steel* audio play to feature Angela Bruce, an actress with numerous screen credits. Though she is probably most famous for her role as Sarah Ling in *Angels* (1978-

1980), she also appeared in the recurring role of Chrissie Stuart in ten episodes of *Press Gang* (1989), including two episodes also featuring David Collings, though they shared no scenes. Bruce has also appeared in genre television, with roles in the *Red Dwarf* episode 'Parallel Universe' (1988) and the *Doctor Who* story 'Battlefield' (1989), and she took the role of Dayna in the *Blake's 7* 'The SevenFold Crown' and 'The Syndeton Experiment' (1998) for BBC Radio.

Overview:
'Zero' sees David Collings and Mark Gatiss thrust centre stage as Silver and Gold, and both get what are now commonly known as 'character arcs'. Although *Sapphire & Steel* was rarely a genuine science fiction series, the story manages to bypass this somewhat by having the space shuttle as the proverbial 'claustrophobic location' and little more. The notion of creatures that can invade the dreams of all humankind is a little farfetched, but this too is diverted by having the plot centre on the politics of the elements and the transient beings, and the interaction between the four leads. Occasionally the dialogue strays into unnaturalistic territory, overt exposition or just plain odd descriptive passages ('It has the smell of despair') but generally this is Lyons' most fleshed-out script for the series. It also contains some interesting speculation about the nature of the agents. In the opening episode, Silver and Gold discuss humanity and refer to it and the Earth as being apart from themselves, clearly suggesting that they are not of this planet. Yet later, Sapphire states that aliens have not been encountered, which would echo the fifth television story's assertion that Sapphire and Steel are only aliens 'in an extraterrestrial sense'. The character of Mercury also gets mentioned, and identified as a male who enjoys playing chess with Silver. Whether or not such revelations are regarded as 'canon' is open to debate, but such character touches add to the flavour of the audio.

Story Fifteen: Wall Of Darkness
Writer: Nigel Fairs
Director: Nigel Fairs
Production: February 2008
Release Date: September 2008

Duration: Four Episodes - 31′ 14″/26′ 36″/25′ 20″/27′ 52″
Additional Cast: Louise Jameson (Sally), Ian Hallard (Justin), Robert Maloney (Russell), Timothy Watson (Jason), Joannah Tincey (Miranda), Lisa Bowerman (Ruby) and Sarah Douglas (Godwin).
Additional Crew: Paul Wilson (Website), John Ainsworth (Marketing & Publicity), Miles Haigh-Ellery/Gary Atterton (Big Finish Administration), Frances Welsh (Producers' Assistant) and David Richardson (Line Producer).

Summary: Sapphire and Steel are sent to investigate a deserted underground shopping mall, all that remains in San Francisco after a nuclear war in 2004. However, they become separated into divergent realities, including one where the war never happened. Just what hold do Sally and her two sons have over the realities, and are Sapphire and Steel really as free as they believe?

Trivia: A collection of clips and outtakes from both the *Sapphire & Steel* and the *Tomorrow People* ranges is included on the first disc, lasting 18′ 21″.

Overview:
The most overtly political story from the audio range, 'Wall of Darkness' features a world ravaged by a nuclear holocaust of America's making. With Louise Jameson excellent in a supporting role, this is an engaging yet never surprising tale that does seem to cover a lot of old ground for the range. It concludes with the previously-explored idea of the two agents being trapped on a compact disc. All three previous stories in the third season featured a 'hidden track' at the end of the disc, consisting of either Warner or Harker speaking a line after a section of silence. This ranged from Warner's 'Hello? If this is some kind of radio drama then presumably someone is listening ... Can you hear me?' to Harker's plaintive 'Steel? It's cold.' This is resumed here with an ambiguous ending that implies the entire final season was a continuing part of the trap - possibly even further - and smacks of 'the toys being placed back in the box'. With this being probably the final *Sapphire & Steel* story from Big Finish, then the series is left where it was taken up: with both Sapphire and Steel trapped forever, with no escape.

INDEX

Numbers in italics indicate credit only entries.

ABOUT THE AUTHOR

Richard Callaghan was terrified of *Sapphire & Steel* as a child and set out to write a book to hopefully reflect what he regarded as an outstanding television programme. Based around the West Midlands area, he can occasionally be seen studying Media.

11657418R00107

Printed in Great Britain
by Amazon.co.uk, Ltd.,
Marston Gate.